First-Time Iowa Travel Tips

Zakariyya .T Dennis

Introduction

Embark on an exciting adventure through Iowa with this book, revealing offbeat destinations that promise unforgettable experiences. From quirky landmarks to natural wonders, Iowa offers a diverse range of attractions for every traveler.

Explore the unique landscapes and climate of Iowa while visiting fascinating sites like Adventureland Park, Ledges State Park, and Okoboji Lake. Encounter whimsical attractions such as Elwood, the World's Tallest Concrete Gnome, and Iowa's Largest Frying Pan.

Delve into history at the Buffalo Bill Museum, National Hobo Museum, and the historic sites of Clear Lake. Discover the charm of Amana Colonies, the artistic scene in Cedar Rapids, and the beauty of Rathbun Lake.

For nature enthusiasts, the Loess Hills, Hitchcock Nature Area, and Maquoketa Caves State Park offer stunning outdoor experiences. Experience the thrill of Roller Coaster Road and the tranquility of Swan Lake.

Uncover hidden gems like the Effigy Mounds National Monument, Field of Dreams Movie Site, and the American Gothic House. Traverse the picturesque High Trestle Trail Bridge, visit the historic town of Elkader, and explore the Devonian Fossil Gorge.

Enjoy family-friendly attractions such as Blank Park Zoo, Saylorville Lake, and the Storybook Hill Children's Zoo. For adventure seekers, Zombie Burger + Drink Lab and Sundown Mountain promise exciting experiences.

Immerse yourself in cultural delights with the Dubuque Symphony Orchestra, the National Mississippi River Museum and Aquarium, and the charming town of Iowa City. Visit iconic landmarks like Kinnick Stadium, the Black Angel of Oakland Cemetery, and the Swinging Bridge.

Whether you're interested in history, outdoor adventures, or unique landmarks, Iowa's diverse attractions are sure to leave you with lasting memories. Grab your bucket list and get ready to explore the hidden treasures of the Hawkeye State!

Contents

About Iowa

Iowa is the home state of many memorable sights and scenes. The state is in between the Mississippi and Missouri rivers and has a population of nearly 3 million people.

Iowa has been populated for about 13,000 years, as American Indians first settled in the area during the Archaic period. The population was highly reliant on agriculture, with corn quickly becoming the most prominent crop.

The Iowa territory was claimed for France following Jacques Marquette and Louis Jolliet's travels through the area in 1673. The property was transferred to Spain before the French and Indian War. Many of the tribes living in the area sold their land in 1832 as part of the Black Hawk Purchase.

Iowa became the 29th state in the Union in 1846. It continues to grow through its vast farming and manufacturing industries.

Landscape and Climate

Iowa's landscape is filled with many rolling hills. The Driftless Area in the northeastern part of the state features many steep ridges and river valleys that did not experience flattening during the glaciation of the last ice age.

Iowa has various lakes throughout its landscape, some of which are man-made. The natural wetlands that once permeated the state have been largely drained.

Much of Iowa's landscape in the past few years has become more urban in nature. The metropolitan area around the capital city of Des Moines has a population of nearly 700,000 people. Iowa is also home to two of the cities that make up the Quad Cities region with

Illinois: Davenport and Bettendorf. Other notable cities around the state include Cedar Rapids, Sioux City, Iowa City, Ames, Dubuque, Mason City, and the Omaha suburb of Council Bluffs.

Iowa is home to a humid continental climate, with temperatures consistent throughout most of the state. Temperatures can reach an average high of about 85°F in the summer and can go as low as 10°F in the winter. Some north-central areas like Mason City can experience temperatures about 5 degrees colder than other parts of the state. Conditions can be very humid throughout the year.

The southeastern ends of the state receive more rainfall each year, with some parts bringing in about 40 inches a year. The northwestern area near Sioux Falls, South Dakota, gets closer to 30 inches annually. The state also gets about 15 to 25 days of snowfall during the winter season.

Site of the First Train Robbery in the West

The first train robbery in the West happened outside of the town of Adair, west of Des Moines. Jesse James and members of his gang robbed a train of $3,000 in currency and other goods on July 21, 1873. The spot would inspire many other outlaws and bandits in the West to start targeting trains.

The site, about 1 mile from Adair, is marked with a distinct train wheel. The wheel stands in the pavement with a small marker on top of it. You'll also find a piece of railroad track.

Best Time to Visit:
The site is open throughout the year.

Pass/Permit/Fees:
There is no cost to visit the site.

Closest City or Town:
Adair

Physical Address:
1156 Anita Adair Rd, Adair, IA 50002

GPS Coordinates:
41.48348° N, 94.67569° W

Did You Know?
You can tell you're in Adair when you see the giant water tower with a yellow paint job and a smiley face.

Adventureland Park

Adventureland Park in Altoona is a family-owned amusement park with more than 50 rides in both the traditional park area and the waterpark region. There are six roller coasters, including the Dragon Slayer, Monster, Outlaw, and Tornado coasters. The Tornado is one of the park's oldest rides, built in 1978. Other rides at the park include Lady Luck, a roulette-themed Trabant ride, and the Red Baron spinning plane ride, where riders can control how high they want to get off the ground. A few of the rides date back to the park's opening in 1974.

Best Time to Visit:
The park operates from April to September. It is open daily in June and July and on weekdays at other points during the season.

Pass/Permit/Fees:
Admission to the park is $50 for an adult or $45 for children and seniors.

Closest City or Town:
Altoona

Physical Address:
3200 Adventureland Dr, Altoona, IA 50009

GPS Coordinates:
41.65817° N, 93.49582° W

Did You Know?
The fastest ride at the park is the Monster, a roller coaster that travels at 65 miles per hour.

Elwood, the World's Tallest Concrete Gnome

You will find Elwood in the southern part of Reiman Gardens at Iowa State University in Ames. Elwood is the world's tallest concrete gnome at about 15 feet in height. He has a distinct red cone hat similar to what you'd find on a lawn gnome. The gnome is also about 3,500 pounds in weight. The gnome was built by artists from the National Rock and Sculpture Center in Wausau, Wisconsin. It is officially listed by Guinness World Records as the tallest gnome, as it is about 2 feet taller than the next one.

Best Time to Visit:
You can visit anytime, but try to come during the spring when the gardens are in bloom.

Pass/Permit/Fees:
Admission to the Reiman Gardens to see Elwood costs $10 for adults and $6 for children.

Closest City or Town:
Ames

Physical Address:
1407 S University Blvd, Ames, IA 50011

GPS Coordinates:
42.00984° N, 93.63922° W

Did You Know?
The gnome and the gardens are south of Jack Trice Stadium, the home of the Iowa State Cyclones college football team.

Ledges State Park

You will find Ledges State Park not far from Ames in north-central Iowa. The park is named for its many limestone ledges, some of which tower 100 feet over the Des Moines River. There are a few cabins, a stone bridge going over Peas Creek, and various owl habitats throughout the park.

The park also houses a 4-mile trail system. Most of the trails are steep, but there's a beginner's trail to the south that leads to nearby Lost Lake at the southern end of the park.

Best Time to Visit:
The fall season is a great time to visit when the fall colors on the trees are on full display.

Pass/Permit/Fees:
The park is free to visit, but it costs extra if you want to reserve one of the camping sites or shelters.

Closest City or Town:
Ames

Physical Address:
1515 P Ave, Madrid, IA 50156

GPS Coordinates:
41.99370° N, 93.87499° W

Did You Know?
The waters around the park are suitable for most activities, including stream fishing and canoeing.

Reed/Niland Corner

The Reed/Niland Corner is a re-creation of the old one-stop travel centers you would have found on the Lincoln and Jefferson highways in the early twentieth century. The corner is near the intersections of US-30 and US-65 in Colo. The corner houses Niland's Café, a historic location known for its classic car displays and its red bench that reads EAT.

The Colo Motel features a six-room space, with many rooms restored to look like they did when the highways opened. You'll also see some original neon signs on display around the corner. The area highlights life during the birth of the highway system.

Best Time to Visit:
You can visit the corner at any time of the year.

Pass/Permit/Fees:
It costs extra to rent a room at the corner or to dine at the restaurant.

Closest City or Town:
Ames

Physical Address:
24 Lincoln Hwy, Colo, IA 50056

GPS Coordinates:
42.02298° N, 93.31067° W

Did You Know?
The café here is noteworthy for its extensive assortment of pies.

Okoboji Lake

Okoboji Lake is divided into two halves in Dickinson County in northwestern Iowa. The lake features the small East Okoboji Lake and the more massive West Okoboji Lake. Both of these are members of the Iowa Great Lakes. This lake features a distinct blue body all around. The blue color throughout the lake comes from its extensive depths, and the natural lighting in the area makes for an exciting site. You'll find some of the tallest peaks in Iowa to the north at the Pikes Peak State Park. You can also visit one of the lakeside attractions at the Arnolds Park Amusement Park to the south.

Best Time to Visit:
The summer season is the busiest time when most of the seasonal businesses in the area are open.

Pass/Permit/Fees:
You can visit the lake for free, although it costs extra to rent a boat or to use any of the local services at the businesses near the lake.

Closest City or Town:
Arnolds Park

Physical Address:
Okoboji Blvd, Milford, IA 51351

GPS Coordinates:
43.35456° N, 95.15709° W

Did You Know?
The lake's name was originally from the Sioux tribe, who had landed in the area at one point.

Albert the Bull

Albert the Bull has been a mascot of sorts for the town of Audubon since he was constructed in 1964. Albert is about 28 feet tall and has a 15-foot span between the tips of his horns. The size makes Albert the world's largest bull.

Albert is made of solid concrete and weighs about 45 tons. The steel used to support his frame came from repurposed former windmills.

Albert features an anatomically correct design. His eyes are brown, as that is the most common color for Hereford bulls.

Best Time to Visit:
The bull is open for visiting throughout the year.

Pass/Permit/Fees:
You can visit the bull for free.

Closest City or Town:
Audubon

Physical Address:
115 Circle Dr, Audubon, IA 50025

GPS Coordinates:
41.71115° N, 94.92608° W

Did You Know?
The most popular part of Albert is that his testicles are clearly visible. Some people have been known to paint them various colors, including blue during the winter.

Buffalo Bill Museum

The Buffalo Bill Museum is in Le Claire, a town northeast of the Quad Cities area. The museum highlights the history of many people from the Quad Cities, including Le Claire native Buffalo Bill Cody. The venue features stories about Cody's life and his unique accomplishments. There is also a section of the museum devoted to James Ryan, a Le Claire native who invented the flight recorder for aviation purposes. The museum contains a one-room schoolhouse exhibit that portrays what a schoolhouse looked like in the early twentieth century. There's also a section in the museum on James Buchanan Eads, an Iowa resident who designed the Mississippi River Bridge in St. Louis.

Best Time to Visit:
The museum has many touring exhibits throughout the year, so check first to see what is appearing here before you arrive.

Pass/Permit/Fees:
Admission is $2 for adults and $1 for children.

Closest City or Town:
Bettendorf

Physical Address:
199 Front St, Le Claire, IA 52753

GPS Coordinates:
41.59892° N, 90.34285° W

Did You Know?
The museum features a paddlewheel that was used on a paddleboat nearly 100 years ago.

Iowa's Largest Frying Pan

The town of Brandon is home to the state's largest frying pan. The pan is about 9 feet wide and 14 feet long when you include the handle. It also weighs about 1,000 pounds. The pan was built for the Cowboy Breakfast Festival in Brandon in 2004.

The pan is not the world's largest, which is about 15 feet in diameter. However, it is a tribute to the many roadside eateries and diners you'll find on Iowa's highways and rural roads.

Best Time to Visit:
The frying pan is easy to spot in the daylight.

Pass/Permit/Fees:
You don't have to pay anything to see the pan.

Closest City or Town:
Brandon

Physical Address:
800-850 Main St, Brandon, IA 52210

GPS Coordinates:
42.31593° N, 92.00723° W

Did You Know?
The pan is large enough to fry more than 500 eggs at a time.

Lake Darling

Lake Darling is a small lake north of IA-1 near the Lake Darling State Park. Lake Darling features about 300 acres of surrounding land and has a maximum depth of about 20 feet.

There is a beach on the southern end, a few hiking trails around the perimeter of the lake, and multiple boating docks on the southern end. You'll find redear sunfish, largemouth bass, and bluegill while fishing here.

Best Time to Visit:
The spring season is a good time since the water temperature is a little more stable at this point. The conditions are ideal for fishing.

Pass/Permit/Fees:
You can visit the lake for free, but you must have a license for fishing if you want to fish here.

Closest City or Town:
Brighton

Physical Address:
Lake Darling Rd, Brighton, IA 52540

GPS Coordinates:
41.20080° N, 91.89531° W

Did You Know?
You can rent a boat here if you don't have one, although you will need to reserve your rental well in advance. The lake is very popular for fishing, and reservations may be limited.

National Hobo Museum

The American hobo was a unique part of Iowa in the nineteenth century, as hobos would often travel around the state looking for various jobs. You can learn about their history at the National Hobo Museum in downtown Britt. The museum features many stories and artifacts about hobos from the Civil War to today. These include stories about their lives, the jobs they would complete, and the extensive ethical code that they would follow when traveling and completing their jobs in many places around the country.

Best Time to Visit:
The museum hosts the National Hobo Convention on the second weekend of August. The event has been held almost every year since 1900.

Pass/Permit/Fees:
It costs $5 to visit the museum.

Closest City or Town:
Britt

Physical Address:
51 Main Ave S, Britt, IA 50423

GPS Coordinates:
43.09645° N, 93.80166° W

Did You Know?
The National Hobo Museum and its included gift shop are inside the Chief Theater, an old movie theater that was built in the early twentieth century.

Shimek State Forest

Shimek State Forest is at the far southeastern end of Iowa, north of the Des Moines River near the Missouri border.

The forest features five units totaling nearly 10,000 acres. You'll find more than 20 hiking trails throughout, many of which go across Lick Creek. There are more than 60 miles of space for hiking, horseback riding, cross-country skiing, and mountain biking. You can also go hunting for small game and wild turkeys, or you can fish for redear sunfish or channel catfish.

Best Time to Visit:
The fall is a good time for hunting or fishing. You'll also love the beautiful colors of the trees during this season.

Pass/Permit/Fees:
You will require a fishing or hunting permit for these activities in the forest.

Closest City or Town:
Burlington

Physical Address:
33653 Rte J56, Farmington, IA 52626

GPS Coordinates:
40.61034° N, 91.68210° W

Did You Know?
The forest was a base for the Civilian Conservation Corps in the 1930s and 1940s.

Snake Alley

Snake Alley is a road in Burlington noted for being one of the world's most crooked streets due to its extremely sharp turns. The road is similar to Lombard Street in San Francisco, but Snake Alley requires a total turning radius of 1,100 degrees versus the 1,000 degrees needed on Lombard Street. Snake Alley is 275 feet long and rises by about 50 feet. It has five half-curves and two quarter curves on its body.

Best Time to Visit:
You'll find many events at Snake Alley throughout the year, including an art festival and a film festival.

Pass/Permit/Fees:
It is free to drive down Snake Alley.

Closest City or Town:
Burlington

Physical Address:
6th St. between Columbia & Washington St, Burlington, IA 52601

GPS Coordinates:
40.81204° N, 91.10577° W

Did You Know?
Snake Alley is a one-way street, as it only goes downhill from north to south. When it was built in 1894, horses often struggled to climb up the road. Therefore, it is a downhill-only road. The road does host an annual uphill-biking event, though.

Swan Lake

Swan Lake is south of the Middle Raccoon River. The lake is in Carroll County and is open for boating and other activities.

Swan Lake features a small series of trails around its border. The end of the Sauk Rail Trail is on the southern part of the lake. The trail goes east to Sac County to Black Hawk Park. There's also a smaller trail at the park that goes along the entire perimeter of the lake. You'll also find stations on the eastern end where you can get a boat ready for sailing.

Best Time to Visit:
The lake waters are their calmest during the summer season.

Pass/Permit/Fees:
You can visit the lake for free.

Closest City or Town:
Carroll

Physical Address:
22676 Swan Lake Trail, Carroll, IA 51401

GPS Coordinates:
42.04085° N, 94.84503° W

Did You Know?
Most of Swan Lake is actually a reservoir. The lake is formed from excess water that comes from the Middle Raccoon River.

Amana Colonies

The seven German villages known as the Amana Colonies are southwest of Cedar Rapids. The villages include various homes and businesses operated by many generations of German Pietists. The Amana Colonies features small shops, art studios, and restaurants that are run by people in the Amana Society. You can tour some of the communal buildings around the area, including some that existed before the colonies evolved into the for-profit Amana Society in 1932. Many of the properties were built by first-generation German immigrants.

Best Time to Visit:
Tours of the communal villages around the Amana Colonies are held from May to October each year.

Pass/Permit/Fees:
622 46th Ave, Amana, IA 52203

Closest City or Town:
Cedar Rapids

Physical Address:
You can reach the Amana Colonies from Cedar Rapids or Iowa City by taking US-151. The colonies are slightly north of the Iowa River.

GPS Coordinates:
41.80030° N, 91.86826° W

Did You Know?
Most of the people living in the colonies speak English, High German, and Amana German.

Brucemore

The Brucemore estate in Cedar Rapids is a Queen Anne–style mansion built in the 1880s. The estate is open for tours. Brucemore has been a hub for the arts over the years. The luxurious house was the home of three different families for a span of over 100 years.

The estate has grown to feature many unique art installations, a few specialty rooms, and an extensive garden. Brucemore hosts many concerts, festivals, and garden programs. There's also an annual outdoor theater program at Brucemore.

Best Time to Visit:
Most of the events at the estate occur during the summer season. Check before visiting to see what is playing here.

Pass/Permit/Fees:
You can visit the estate for free during grounds hours. You will require a ticket for a tour or other special event. The price will vary by event.

Closest City or Town:
Cedar Rapids

Physical Address:
2160 Linden Dr. SE, Cedar Rapids, IA 52403

GPS Coordinates:
41.99101° N, 91.63511° W

Did You Know?
The sleeping porch on the property was designed by Grant Wood.

Cedar Rapids

Cedar Rapids is the second-most populated city in Iowa, with a population of about 130,000 people. This city is located in Linn County on the Cedar River. Cedar Rapids is home to one of the country's largest Czech and Slovak populations. The Czech Village neighborhood features many Czech businesses and shops. The Czech & Slovak Museum & Library is located here and features many artifacts relating to these countries. The Hotel Roosevelt in downtown Cedar Rapids is one of the top sites in the city. The old hotel has become a vital commercial center in the heart of the city.

Best Time to Visit:
The city has a farmers' market that operates in the morning hours during select weekends throughout the year.

Pass/Permit/Fees:
You can visit the city for free.

Closest City or Town:
Cedar Rapids

Physical Address:
370 1st Ave E, Cedar Rapids, IA 52401

GPS Coordinates:
41.97587° N, 91.66536° W

Did You Know?
Cedar Rapids is home to the National Muslim Cemetery, which became the country's first Muslim cemetery when it opened in 1948. All the graves face in the direction of Mecca.

National Czech & Slovak Museum & Library

The National Czech and Slovak Museum and Library in Cedar Rapids is a Smithsonian-affiliated museum highlighting the history of the Czech Republic and Slovakia. This museum houses a collection of many texts, recordings, and films from the peoples of these two countries. There are exhibits about the evolution of the Czech Republic and Slovakia. You will find works of art and clothing on display, plus rotating exhibits showing unique parts of the area's history. The museum has housed some artifacts from the National Museum in Prague in the past.

Best Time to Visit:
Check with the museum to see which traveling exhibits are on display before visiting.

Pass/Permit/Fees:
Admission is $10 for adults and $5 for children.

Closest City or Town:
Cedar Rapids

Physical Address:
1400 Inspiration Pl SW, Cedar Rapids, IA 52404

GPS Coordinates:
41.96640° N, 91.66166° W

Did You Know?
Presidents Bill Clinton, Vaclav Havel, and Michal Kovac dedicated the museum in 1995.

Rathbun Lake

Rathbun Lake is in Appanoose County at the southern end of the state near the Chariton River. Rathbun Lake was formed by a dam constructed in the 1960s. The lake features various wildlife for fishing and hunting activities. You'll find Canada geese, wild turkeys, bald eagles, and channel catfish throughout the area.

This location also features an indoor water park, a golf course, and a resort. The Honey Creek State Park Resort is at the eastern end of the lake and is Iowa's first state-run resort.

Best Time to Visit:
The summer is a good time for visiting if you're looking for a space without too many hunters.

Pass/Permit/Fees:
You will require a permit for fishing or hunting in the area. You can also reserve a room at the resort, but it will cost extra.

Closest City or Town:
Centerville

Physical Address:
12633 Resort Dr, Moravia, IA 52571

GPS Coordinates:
40.89563° N, 92.91893° W

Did You Know?
President Richard Nixon spoke at the dedication ceremony for the lake in 1971.

Charles City Whitewater Park

Charles City Whitewater Park is the first of its kind in Iowa since it opened in 2011. Located in the northeastern town of Charles City, this park features many rafting opportunities along the Cedar River. The whitewater park is a portion of Riverfront Park, a venue offering a stone performance theater, a disc golf course, and a play area. You can take a tube or canoe and paddle down the rapids at the park. Stand-up paddle boating is also open in some of the quieter parts. The venue provides a unique opportunity for people to enjoy the sport of whitewater rafting and paddling.

Best Time to Visit:
The park hosts the Iowa Games and Charles City Challenge in the summer.

Pass/Permit/Fees:
It is free to visit the park, but it costs extra to rent a tube or canoe. You can rent one of these from the businesses in the local area.

Closest City or Town:
Charles City

Physical Address:
106 Chapel Ln, Charles City, IA 50616

GPS Coordinates:
43.06466° N, 92.67704° W

Did You Know?
The water at the park features a gentle flow with depths of just a few feet on average.

Villisca Ax Murder House

The Villisca Ax Murder House is the place of one of the most shocking crimes in Iowa history. The home in the southwestern town of Villisca was the site of a murder on June 9, 1912. Six members of the family who owned the property and two guests were killed in the house that night. They all had massive head wounds produced by an ax. The house was restored to its condition in 1912. You can tour the house and learn about where the murders took place and the stories behind the victims. You'll also learn about the investigation into the murders, which are still unsolved to this day.

Best Time to Visit:
The house is popular for visits during the Halloween season.

Pass/Permit/Fees:
Day tours cost $10 per person. You can also reserve an overnight stay at the house for up to six people for $428, plus $75 for each additional person.

Closest City or Town:
Clarinda

Physical Address:
508 E 2nd St, Villisca, IA 50864

GPS Coordinates:
40.93083° N, 94.97328° W

Did You Know?
There have been suggestions over the years that the house may be haunted by the spirits of the eight murder victims.

Buddy Holly Crash Site

The Buddy Holly Crash Site is a few miles north of Clear Lake. This spot is where the iconic rock musician and fellow performers Ritchie Valens and the Big Bopper died in a plane crash on February 3, 1959.

The crash site features a memorial dedicated to the three musicians and the pilot who died in the plane crash. The memorial is composed of a stainless steel guitar with three vinyl records. You'll also find an oversized model of Holly's eyeglasses near the crash site.

Best Time to Visit:
The site is open year-round, although it is especially busy around February 3.

Pass/Permit/Fees:
You can visit the site for free.

Closest City or Town:
Clear Lake

Physical Address:
22728 Gull Avenue, Clear Lake, IA 50428

GPS Coordinates:
43.22052° N, 93.38138° W

Did You Know?
Some clean pieces of laundry are often strung along the marker in reference to Holly wanting to fly to his next show so that he could have extra time to take care of his laundry.

Clear Lake

You'll find Iowa's Clear Lake near the town of the same name in Cerro Gordo. Clear Lake covers about 3,700 acres of land. The lake features a few beach areas with some boating docks on the northern and eastern ends. Clear Lake is popular for yachting, as it is home to a yacht club.

Other features include a wildlife-management area to the west and a golf club to the north. There are also a few small islands around the shores of the lake.

Best Time to Visit:
The summer is optimal yachting season. Yacht and catamaran charters are open during the season.

Pass/Permit/Fees:
You can visit the lake for free, although it will cost extra for you to rent a vessel for travel.

Closest City or Town:
Clear Lake

Physical Address:
6490 S Shore Ct, Clear Lake, IA 50428

GPS Coordinates:
43.12621° N, 93.42079° W

Did You Know?
The Surf Ballroom is near the northeastern part of the lake. This music venue is where Buddy Holly performed his final concert in 1959.

Surf Ballroom and Museum

The Surf Ballroom and Museum in Clear Lake is a performing arts venue that has been in operation since 1948. The ballroom is famous for being where Buddy Holly performed on February 2, 1959. He and a few other performers died in a nearby plane crash the next day.

The venue features a museum highlighting the many acts that have played here. You'll also find a backstage area that has walls covered with autographs from performers.

Best Time to Visit:
The ballroom hosts a Winter Dance Party tribute show every February to honor the stars that played during that 1959 show.

Pass/Permit/Fees:
You can visit the ballroom for free, but a $5 donation is recommended.

Closest City or Town:
Clear Lake

Physical Address:
460 N Shore Dr, Clear Lake, IA 50428

GPS Coordinates:
43.14002° N, 93.38992° W

Did You Know?
The exterior of the Surf Ballroom hasn't been altered much since its opening. The design makes it look like it did back in 1959.

Lake Icaria

Lake Icaria is in Adams County near IA-148 in the town of Corning. The lake features 650 acres of surrounding land and reaches up to 35 feet in depth. The lake flows into the Kempt Creek at the northern and southern ends.

Most of the action on Lake Icaria is in its central part. You'll find a marina here and a nonprimitive campground. You can go fishing for walleye, channel catfish, and perch.

Best Time to Visit:
The waters are their calmest during the spring season.

Pass/Permit/Fees:
You can enter the area for free, but you must have a license for fishing in Iowa.

Closest City or Town:
Corning

Physical Address:
1730 Juniper Ave, Corning, IA 50841

GPS Coordinates:
41.06073° N, 94.72665° W

Did You Know?
The lake didn't exist until the 1970s when a dam was constructed as part of the Watershed Protection and Flood Prevention Act.

Historic Squirrel Cage Jail

The Squirrel Cage Jail is a unique property in Council Bluffs that was built in 1885. The building was used as Pottawattamie County's jail until 1969. The property has developed notoriety over the years due to stories about the inhumane treatment of criminals, and parts of the property have been condemned.

You can visit the unique lazy-Susan-like mechanism of the jail today, a rotating design where a jailer can turn a hand crank to rotate the jail cells, providing easy access to whatever criminals one wanted to contact. The jail cells are still intact and designed to their original specifications.

Best Time to Visit:
The jail is open throughout the year.

Pass/Permit/Fees:
The jail costs $7 to visit.

Closest City or Town:
Council Bluffs

Physical Address:
226 Pearl St, Council Bluffs, IA 51503

GPS Coordinates:
41.25854° N, 95.85191° W

Did You Know?
There were 18 jails of this design scattered around the United States, but only a few of them are still standing today. None of those jails are still in active use, but they are open for tours.

Lake Manawa

Lake Manawa is located at the southern end of Council Bluffs. You'll find it to the east of Omaha's Henry Doorly Zoo. The lake features nearly 750 acres of space.

This is the closest lake to the Omaha–Council Bluffs area that motor boating and water skiing are permitted. You will find multiple fishing and boating areas throughout the southern end of the lake. The north also features a few hiking trails and a golf course. You'll be able to see a few villas to the south.

Best Time to Visit:
The summer is the most active time on the lake, as there are more boats available for rent.

Pass/Permit/Fees:
You can rent a boat at the lake, but the cost will vary depending on the season and the type of boat.

Closest City or Town:
Council Bluffs

Physical Address:
Mohawk St, Council Bluffs, IA 51501

GPS Coordinates:
41.21254° N, 95.84655° W

Did You Know?
The lake was formed in 1881 following a flood in the nearby Missouri River. Much of the water came from Indian Creek, which moves west of the lake.

Loess Hills

The Loess Hills are at the western end of Iowa on the Missouri River. They feature many deposits of loess soil that have been brought over the years by wind. Many of the hills are about 200 feet high over the plains, providing exciting views of the Missouri River and the local wildlife.

The hills produce a drift layer close to 90 feet deep. The layer is created due to its hard surface when dry that becomes moist and fluid when wet.

Best Time to Visit:
The summer is an ideal time to visit when conditions are better on the hills.

Pass/Permit/Fees:
You can visit the area for free, although it helps to visit the main entry point in Pisgah.

Closest City or Town:
Council Bluffs

Physical Address:
206 Polk St, Pisgah, IA 51564

GPS Coordinates:
41.83193° N, 95.92641° W

Did You Know?
The Loess Hills date to the last ice age when sediment and melted water from the area moved into the Missouri River millions of years ago. The sediment produced mud flats that were eventually exposed over time.

Hitchcock Nature Area

You will find the Hitchcock Nature Area in the Loess Hills area of Iowa near Council Bluffs and Omaha, Nebraska. The region features about 1,200 acres of land for camping, hiking, and birding.

There are many deep loess deposits around the Hitchcock Nature Area, some of which are 200 feet deep. The park has a 10-mile trail system available for hiking and cross-country skiing. You can also try your shot at the archery range, although you must bring your own equipment.

Best Time to Visit:
Visit between September and December, as many hawks and other birds of prey will migrate south through the area during that interval.

Pass/Permit/Fees:
You can visit the area for free, but it costs $5 to park, and exact change is required.

Closest City or Town:
Crescent

Physical Address:
27792 Ski Hill Loop, Honey Creek, IA 51542

GPS Coordinates:
41.41512° N, 95.85662° W

Did You Know?
The nature area is close to the Mount Crescent Ski Area, which is open during the winter season and a good place to stop before or after a visit to Hitchcock.

Roller Coaster Road

Roller Coaster Road is in the northeastern end of Iowa near Waterville and Harpers Ferry. This road between Elon Drive and Gronna Drive lasts a few miles and features a distinct path with rolling hills all around.

Roller Coaster Road contains multiple peaks and valleys as you drive north or south. The design makes it look like a roller coaster. The layout provides a fun way for people to travel down the road, but it is also designed to contour along with the natural land masses around the area.

Best Time to Visit:
Visit during the daytime, as there are no lights on the road.

Pass/Permit/Fees:
You can travel the road for free.

Closest City or Town:
Dalby

Physical Address:
Roller Coaster Road, Harpers Ferry, Iowa 52146

GPS Coordinates:
43.25338° N, 91.25032° W

Did You Know?
You'll notice multiple corn fields alongside the road. The corn fields are also designed to contour with the road, producing a roller coaster look to the landscape. The electric poles nearby are placed evenly to keep them looking consistent.

Bellevue State Park

Bellevue State Park overlooks the Mississippi River near the Illinois border. It is divided into two separate units, with the Nelson unit to the north and the Dyas unit southward. The park is home to a butterfly sanctuary. You will find many unique butterflies and a diverse array of flowers and trees throughout the area. There's also an enclosed nature center at the park. You'll find a primitive lime kiln off the Quarry Trail, one of the most popular hiking trails at the park. You can also go hunting on hundreds of acres of public land near the Nelson unit.

Best Time to Visit:
The park is great to visit during the fall when the autumn colors start to appear.

Pass/Permit/Fees:
It is free to visit, but it costs extra to reserve a camping site. Camping is only open at the Dyas unit. You must also acquire a license if you want to hunt on the grounds near the Nelson unit.

Closest City or Town:
Dubuque

Physical Address:
24668 US-52, Bellevue, IA 52031

GPS Coordinates:
42.25661° N, 90.41993° W

Did You Know?
There are close to 60 species of butterfly present in the park garden.

Iowa 80 Trucking Museum

The town of Walcott outside of Davenport is home to the Iowa 80 truck stop, the world's largest. You'll find the Iowa 80 Trucking Museum in the northern part of the truck-stop complex.

The museum features many old trucks on display, including a few from the 1920s and 1930s. The museum also displays antique toy trucks and some old filling station equipment and designs. You'll find antique metal signs taken from many of the oldest filling stations from around the country.

The museum also has a theater that shows short films about trucking and its history.

Best Time to Visit:
The museum is open year-round.

Pass/Permit/Fees:
The museum is free to visit.

Closest City or Town:
Davenport

Physical Address:
505 Sterling Dr, Walcott, IA 52773

GPS Coordinates:
41.62091° N, 90.78138° W

Did You Know?
The 1903 Eldridge truck is the oldest one you will find at the museum. The truck is designed to look like an old farm wagon, and it only goes about 10 miles per hour.

Makoqueta Caves State Park

Makoqueta Caves State Park is a historic park north of the eastern town of Makoqueta. The park has more caves than any other state park in Iowa. It features many bluffs throughout the area, plus 6 miles of trail space. The caves offer limestone formations and various bluffs surrounding the space. The surfaces include stalactites appearing in some of the caves, although a few of the formations have been impacted by visitors. You will also find some chimneys and arches inside the caves here.

Best Time to Visit:
The summer is a good time to visit, as the caves offer comfortable temperatures then.

Pass/Permit/Fees:
The park is free to visit, but it may cost extra to access some areas depending on the season.

Closest City or Town:
Davenport

Physical Address:
9688 Caves Rd, Maquoketa, IA 52060

GPS Coordinates:
42.12196° N, 90.76543° W

Did You Know?
The park offers a white noise syndrome program during the summer season. White noise syndrome often impacts the bats inside the cave, as they can develop white growths on their wings.

West Lake Beach

West Lake Beach offers a beautiful respite from the bustle of the nearby Quad Cities, about 10 miles west of Davenport.

The beach surrounds the Lake of the Hills. It offers a disc golf course and a few campsites. The area is a fun place for swimming, and there is a rinsing shower available. The water is tested each week for safety.

Best Time to Visit:
The beach is open from Memorial Day to Labor Day.

Pass/Permit/Fees:
Daily beach access is $4 for adults and $3 for children. A season pass for the entire family is available for $120 each year.

Closest City or Town:
Davenport

Physical Address:
14910 110th Avenue Gate 1, Davenport, IA 52804

GPS Coordinates:
41.52332° N, 90.67912° W

Did You Know?
The beach is open for various events, including family reunions, corporate business meetings, and other activities. Alcohol is not allowed at any time.

Wildcat Den Trail

The Wildcat Den Trail is in Wildcat Den State Park, north of the Mississippi River near the Illinois border. The trail is 4 miles long and goes through most parts of the park.

This trail features many wildflowers, and the path and bluffs provide exciting views of the land near the river. Some of the cliffs around the trail are about 75 feet high.

You'll also find a few well-preserved buildings along this route, including an old mill. The Pine Creek Grist Mill is on the eastern end of the trail, featuring an original 1878 bridge. This is the only bridge connected to a mill in the state.

Best Time to Visit:
The weather conditions are at their best from March to October.

Pass/Permit/Fees:
The trail is open for free.

Closest City or Town:
Davenport

Physical Address:
1884 Wildcat Den Rd, Muscatine, IA52761

GPS Coordinates:
41.46843° N, 90.87423° W

Did You Know?
Much of the trail goes over Pine Creek. The eastern end of the creek directly flows into the Mississippi River.

Decorah

Decorah is in Winneshiek County in northeastern Iowa. The town is noted for its strong Norwegian-American population, as many Norwegians started settling in the area in the 1850s. The Vesterheim Norwegian-American Museum is located here as well. The Upper Iowa River goes through the middle of Decorah, linking it to many popular natural sites, including Dunnings Spring Park and the Upper Iowa River Access Area.

Best Time to Visit:
Nordic Fest occurs in Decorah every July. The festival highlights Norwegian culture and offers a food show and ethnic dancing performances.

Pass/Permit/Fees:
You can visit Decorah for free, but there may be charges for admission to some sites.

Closest City or Town:
Decorah

Physical Address:
507 W Water St, Decorah, IA 52101

GPS Coordinates:
43.30476° N, 91.79150° W

Did You Know?
Decorah is home to a crater underneath the town that is about 4 miles wide. The crater was produced by a meteorite that crashed into the area about 470 million years ago, suggesting that a massive space rock may have broken up and impacted many parts of Earth back then.

Dunning Springs Decorah

You'll find a 200-foot waterfall at the Dunning's Spring Park in Decorah. The park is north of the Upper Iowa River and features 115 acres of space.

You'll find the waterfall a few hundred yards from the parking lot. The waterfall is picturesque in many directions as it slowly descends from the top.

There's also an ice cave near the parking area. The cave features a few dark spaces with many small rock formations.

Best Time to Visit:
The summer is a great time to visit. The ice cave and the waters from the waterfall produce a cool atmosphere.

Pass/Permit/Fees:
The park is free to visit.

Closest City or Town:
Decorah

Physical Address:
Ice Cave Rd, Decorah, IA 52101

GPS Coordinates:
43.31239° N, 91.79010° W

Did You Know?
You can see Antero Island through some parts of the park area. The island is in the middle of the Upper Iowa River.

Malanaphy Spring Falls

You'll find the Malanaphy Spring Falls near the northern end of the Upper Iowa River Access Area outside Decorah in the northern part of the state. The waterfall is about 1 mile from the parking area.

There is a series of rock formations by the waterfall, with many of the formations featuring native grasses and mosses hanging from the sides. The spring-fed waterfall produces chilly water throughout the year, and the water at the bottom is shallow enough to enjoy wading in the space.

The top of the waterfall is close to 50 feet. You can climb to the top if you wish, but be sure when doing so that the footing is safe to traverse.

Best Time to Visit:
The summer is the perfect time to visit the cool spring falls.

Pass/Permit/Fees:
The waterfall area is free to visit.

Closest City or Town:
Decorah

Physical Address:
2820 Bluffton Rd, Decorah, IA 52101

GPS Coordinates:
43.34535° N, 91.84310° W

Did You Know?
The waterfall is also close to Decorah Ice Cave, another popular attraction in the area.

Siewers Springs

You will find one of the most distinct cascades in Iowa at Siewers Springs in Decorah. The cascade is near the Decorah Fish Hatchery and features one of the most unique designs among waterfalls in the state.

The hatchery is noteworthy for being a site where fish are raised for transport to Iowa's many ponds and lakes. Still, the waterfalls at Siewers Springs are the most popular attraction to see.

You will find multiple rock tiers where the water cascades at Siewers Springs. The tiers produce a staircase formation with a hiking space where you can reach the top.

Best Time to Visit:
The spring and summer are the best times to visit the springs.

Pass/Permit/Fees:
You can visit the springs for free.

Closest City or Town:
Decorah

Physical Address:
2325 Siewers Spring Rd, Decorah, IA 52101

GPS Coordinates:
43.27388° N, 91.78107° W

Did You Know?
The hatchery houses a variety of fish that you can find in several bodies of water throughout the state.

Upper Iowa River

The Upper Iowa River is a tributary of the Mississippi River in the far northeastern part of the state. The tributary is about 150 miles long and goes through four Iowa counties and another in Minnesota.

Much of the Upper Iowa River was formed after the last ice age, as it was not covered in glacial drift. The area features many high-wall canyons and bluffs that you can visit during a canoe ride. You will also find various forms of native vegetation throughout this picturesque part of the state.

Best Time to Visit:
The spring and summer are good times to visit, as the water conditions will not be too chilly during those seasons.

Pass/Permit/Fees:
The lake is free to visit throughout the year.

Closest City or Town:
Decorah

Physical Address:
2820 Bluffton Rd, Decorah, IA 52101

GPS Coordinates:
43.43369° N, 91.84753° W

Did You Know?
The Upper Iowa River is home to many migrating birds, including turkey vultures and bald eagles. Many of these birds can be found closer to the river basin.

Big Creek State Park

Big Creek State Park is near Saylorville Lake, about 20 miles north of Des Moines. The park surrounds the Big Creek Lake and features the largest state-operated beach.

In addition to the beach at the northern end, the southern part of the park offers a disc golf course. You can also travel on the Neil Smith Trail, which runs 27 miles from the beach and eventually reaches downtown Des Moines.

You'll find multiple boating ramps at all ends of the park. There are five ramps that will lead you to the water, but you can also go fishing off of jetties in the area.

Best Time to Visit:
The park is popular during the summer season.

Pass/Permit/Fees:
The park is free to visit, but it costs extra to rent a boat or to get access to a boating ramp or campsite.

Closest City or Town:
Des Moines

Physical Address:
8794 NW 125th Ave, Polk City, IA 50226

GPS Coordinates:
41.79365° N, 93.73352° W

Did You Know?
You'll come across the Tournament Club of Iowa to the south of the park. The golf course is the only Arnold Palmer–designed course in the state.

Blank Park Zoo

The Blank Park Zoo in Des Moines is the only zoo in Iowa to be accredited by the Association of Zoos and Aquariums. It features about 1,500 animals from more than 100 species. The zoo houses many sections devoted to animals from around the world, including animals from Africa and Australia. There's also a tropical aviary housing many unique birds. The Big Cat Complex contains animals such as the snow leopard and African lion. There's also an aquarium featuring various fish from different coral reefs from around the world.

Best Time to Visit:
The zoo hosts many special events throughout the year, including a few holiday-themed events in November and December.

Pass/Permit/Fees:
Admission is $14 for adults and $8 for children.

Closest City or Town:
Des Moines

Physical Address:
7401 SW 9th St, Des Moines, IA 50315

GPS Coordinates:
41.52082° N, 93.62509° W

Did You Know?
The Blank Park name comes from Myron Blank, a movie theater chain owner who helped endow the zoo. Blank is most noteworthy for helping popularize popcorn as a movie theater snack.

Des Moines Art Center

The Des Moines Art Center is one of the capital city's most popular attractions, housing a vast collection of paintings from around the world. It offers paintings from Cassatt, Wood, Hopper, Warhol, Monet, and Lichtenstein.

The art center itself features an Art Deco–inspired structure built in the 1940s. It also features a Modernist addition, designed by I. M. Pei in the 1960s.

There are various touring exhibits throughout the year and an on-site restaurant called Tangerine.

Best Time to Visit:
The art center hosts many touring exhibits, so check to see what is showing here before you arrive.

Pass/Permit/Fees:
The museum is free to visit.

Closest City or Town:
Des Moines

Physical Address:
4700 Grand Ave, Des Moines, IA 50312

GPS Coordinates:
41.58427° N, 93.68117° W

Did You Know?
Edward Hopper's 1927 painting *Automat* is one of the most prominent works on display at the museum. The painting features a woman who Hopper modeled after his wife.

Elk Rock State Park

You'll find Elk Rock State Park about 40 miles southeast of Des Moines. The park is on Lake Red Rock, the state's largest body of water. Rock formations appear around the southern end of the lake, which you can view along the nearly 13 miles of trail space throughout the park. The park features enough room for horseback riding, mountain biking, and hiking. You can also go snowmobiling or cross-country skiing during the winter. A boat launching area is near the southern central part of the lake. You can go fishing for channel catfish, bluegill, and many other fish.

Best Time to Visit:
The summer is a great time for fishing here.

Pass/Permit/Fees:
It costs extra to reserve a camping site at the park. You'll also require a permit if you wish to hunt in the designated spots around the park during the proper season.

Closest City or Town:
Des Moines

Physical Address:
811 146th Ave, Knoxville, IA 50138

GPS Coordinates:
41.40102° N, 93.06318° W

Did You Know?
You can see more of the lake from the Cordova Observation Tower to the north of the park. The tower is close to 100 feet in height.

Green Valley State Park

Green Valley State Park is about 65 miles southwest of Des Moines. The park is in a region featuring four separate lakes within 10 miles of one another.

You'll find 10 miles of trails at the park, and you can go fishing at Green Valley Lake for channel catfish, walleye, and bluegill. The park also has designated areas for water-skiing.

Green Valley Dam is located at the southern end of the park. The dam is responsible for the creation of Green Valley Lake.

Best Time to Visit:
The spring is the best time to visit, as you can see the trees in bloom.

Pass/Permit/Fees:
Admission to the park is free, but it costs extra to reserve a campsite or use the boating dock.

Closest City or Town:
Des Moines

Physical Address:
1480 130th St, Creston, IA 50801

GPS Coordinates:
41.11483° N, 94.38112° W

Did You Know?
You can find bobcats and various other wildlife around the park throughout the year.

Pappajohn Sculpture Park

The Des Moines Art Center operates the Pappajohn Sculpture Park in downtown Des Moines. The park covers 4 acres of land and features sculptures from artists like Ai Weiwei, Jaume Plensa, and Barry Flanagan.

Among the most popular sculptures here include Yoshitomo *Nara's White Ghost* and Yayoi Kusama's *Pumpkin Large*. Kusama's pumpkin is about 8 feet in height. You'll also notice the tricolor *Three Dancing Figures* sculpture by Keith Haring at the park.

Best Time to Visit:
Visit during the summer when the sculptures won't be covered with leaves or ice.

Pass/Permit/Fees:
Like the Des Moines Art Center, the park is free to visit.

Closest City or Town:
Des Moines

Physical Address:
1330 Grand Ave, Des Moines, IA 50309

GPS Coordinates:
41.58586° N, 93.63529° W

Did You Know?
One of the sculptures at the park is a replica of Robert Indiana's *Love* pop art sculpture. While the original is in Indianapolis, this is an exact replica. The sculpture is one of the most iconic pieces of pop art in history.

Saylorville Lake

Saylorville Lake is at the northwestern end of Des Moines. The lake forms from the Des Moines River and flows upstream from the city. It was created to prevent flooding in the river and to control potential flood crests in the Mississippi River.

Saylorville Lake features a butterfly garden at the southeastern end. There are also multiple camping sites and trails in the central area. The lake's marina is to the northeast. Game bird hunting and disc golf are among the most popular activities here.

Best Time to Visit:
The fall season is an ideal time for visiting, as the water is calm, and you'll start to notice the beautiful fall colors around the lake.

Pass/Permit/Fees:
The lake is free to visit, although you'll need a permit for fishing or hunting if you want to do either here.

Closest City or Town:
Des Moines

Physical Address:
Parking lot, 5798 NW 98th Ave, Polk City, IA 50226

GPS Coordinates:
41.74288° N, 93.69361° W

Did You Know?
The dam that forms the lake is one of the largest in the state at slightly less than 7,000 feet long.

State Capitol

The Iowa State Capitol in Des Moines is a Renaissance Revival dome building that was constructed in the 1880s. The Capitol houses the state's General Assembly and the office of many political figures. This building features five separate domes, with the central dome covered in a thin layer of 23-carat gold. The inside contains wood materials from various Iowan forests.

You can tour the Capitol and see the many places where the state's government operates. You'll also learn about the World Food Prize, a ceremony held at the Capitol each year to honor people who make food available to different parts of the world.

Best Time to Visit:
The Capitol is open from Monday to Saturday.

Pass/Permit/Fees:
Tours of the Capitol are free.

Closest City or Town:
Des Moines

Physical Address:
1007 E Grand Ave, Des Moines, IA 50319

GPS Coordinates:
41.59188° N, 93.60385° W

Did You Know?
The building has a chamber for the Iowa Supreme Court, although most of the court's activities are instead held at a nearby building.

Zombie Burger + Drink Lab

People looking for a more interesting place to dine while in Des Moines will find Zombie Burger to be an entertaining place. The "*gore*met" diner is heavily influenced by roadside burger stands and makes its burgers with a three-cut beef blend.

Zombie Burger offers many zombie-themed burgers, including the bacon and egg Dawn of the Dead burger and the Walking Ched burger with deep-fried macaroni. The Undead Elvis burger also features peanut butter and banana. The Drink Lab includes many zombie-themed cocktails and "monster mules." There's also a shake lab that offers some fun combinations.

Best Time to Visit:
The venue is most popular on the weekends.

Pass/Permit/Fees:
Most diners will eat for about $10 to $15 on average, although that total will be higher for alcohol purchases.

Closest City or Town:
Des Moines

Physical Address:
300 E Grand Ave, Des Moines, IA 50309

GPS Coordinates:
41.59118° N, 93.61341° W

Did You Know?
You can spike a shake with alcohol if you wish.

Bonnie and Clyde Dexter Shootout Marker

Bonnie Parker and Clyde Barrow camped in an abandoned amusement park in the town of Dexter near the South Raccoon River in 1933. You'll find a small marker noting where the shootout occurred in Dexter. The marker lists where Bonnie and Clyde and a few members of their gang hid. They stayed in the area on July 23, 1933, and were caught in an ambush by local police. Bonnie, Clyde, and another member of their party escaped the shootout and would continue to rob banks and other places until their deaths a year later.

Best Time to Visit:
The shootout marker is open throughout the year.

Pass/Permit/Fees:
You can visit the area for free.

Closest City or Town:
Dexter

Physical Address:
3291 Dexfield Rd, Dexter, IA 50070

GPS Coordinates:
41.56348° N, 94.23380° W

Did You Know?
Bonnie, Clyde, and their gang hid in the area to recover from injuries sustained in a shootout they escaped in Missouri. One person died a few days later, and they were located after some bloodied bandages were found nearby.

Okomanpeedan Lake

Okomanpeedan Lake has 2,300 acres of space formed on the east fork of the Des Moines River. Much of the lake is in the northern end of Iowa, but most of its mass is in Minnesota.

You'll find dozens of camping sites, plus a few boat launching spots here. You can fish for bullhead, catfish, crappie, and northern pike as well.

Best Time to Visit:
The summer season is the best time to visit when the weather is more temperate.

Pass/Permit/Fees:
You can visit for free, but you will need a fishing license if you want to fish here. You may require a license for both Iowa and Minnesota fishing, depending on where you intend to fish.

Closest City or Town:
Dolliver

Physical Address:
5118 Tuttle Lake Rd, Dolliver, IA 50531

GPS Coordinates:
43.49228° N, 94.58523° W

Did You Know?
The lake's official name is the Okamanpeedan Lake, which comes from the Native American term for "nesting site for herons." But the lake is also known as Tuttle Lake. That name comes from Calvin Tuttle, the first settler on the lake.

Bell Tower Theater

The Bell Tower Theater in Dubuque is a small theater that can accommodate about 300 patrons for shows. The theater produces various plays and musicals each year, as well as assorted family-friendly events. There are also many seasonal events that occur during the Christmas holiday.

The Bell Tower Theater offers a kids' program in the summer, helping them learn about performing arts, music, and other concepts. The programs are available to grade-school children and to preschool kids alike.

Best Time to Visit:
The theater has a regular schedule of shows each year. Check with the theater to see what is playing here before you visit.

Pass/Permit/Fees:
Admission to a show will vary by program.

Closest City or Town:
Dubuque

Physical Address:
2728 Asbury Rd # 242, Dubuque, IA 52001

GPS Coordinates:
42.50958° N, 90.70841° W

Did You Know?
The building that houses the theater was used as a church when it was built in 1930.

Crystal Lake Cave

The Crystal Lake Cave in Dubuque was discovered in 1868 and features many natural crystal formations. This cave contains various unique crystals like aragonite and stalactite. The cave is well lit and has various curves and turns. You will find many small openings with one-of-a-kind crystal formations and shapes formed over thousands of years. The cave also has a gem-mining area for kids. Young visitors can learn how geology works and how miners look for crystals and other items.

Best Time to Visit:
The cave is open throughout the summer. It is also open during the other three seasons, but its hours aren't as extensive.

Pass/Permit/Fees:
Tickets are $20 for adults and $8 for children.

Closest City or Town:
Dubuque

Physical Address:
6684 Crystal Lake Cave Rd, Dubuque, IA 52003

GPS Coordinates:
42.43446° N, 90.62110° W

Did You Know?
Temperatures are relatively cool inside the cave throughout much of the year. The cave's depth and natural insulation allow it to stay comfortable, although a light jacket is recommended when visiting the venue.

Dubuque Symphony Orchestra

The Dubuque Symphony Orchestra has been entertaining the Dubuque area with classical music performances since 1957. The orchestra features a full arrangement that hosts many events throughout the year. The highlight of the orchestra's annual calendar is its Christmas shows in December. The orchestra also offers many themed concerts that feature music from various eras in history.

Many of the orchestra's shows are performed at the Dubuque Arboretum and the Five Flags Theater. Members of the orchestra also perform various shows at the Mississippi Moon Bar at the Diamond Jo Casino complex.

Best Time to Visit:
The schedule for shows changes throughout the year.

Pass/Permit/Fees:
The cost for tickets to a show will vary by performance.

Closest City or Town:
Dubuque

Physical Address:
2728 Asbury Rd #900, Dubuque, IA 52001

GPS Coordinates:
42.50984° N, 90.70867° W

Did You Know?
The orchestra is always looking for members, as it hosts auditions throughout the year for performers in many classes. These include woodwind, cello, and bass performers, among others.

Dubuque Water Trail

You can paddle down the Mississippi River in a kayak or canoe on the Dubuque Water Trail. The trail is about 11 miles long and features five entry points, starting from the north at McDonald Park and south at Massey Marina Park.

The trail goes along various small islands in the middle of the Mississippi River. It also offers fishing access throughout many spots. Most of the entry points for the trail are near park spaces like the Miller Riverview Park and Mines of Spain recreation area.

Best Time to Visit:
The fall is a beautiful time to visit. You'll find impressive views of the trees as they change colors for the season.

Pass/Permit/Fees:
It may cost money to rent a canoe or kayak to reach the trail. You must also have a license for fishing in Iowa if you want to fish on the trail.

Closest City or Town:
Dubuque

Physical Address:
9526 Massey Station Rd, Dubuque, IA 52003

GPS Coordinates:
42.43294° N, 90.58603° W

Did You Know?
You'll find a 5-mile paddling loop near the Catfish Creek park space.

Eagle Point Park

You can see the Mississippi River from many spots at Eagle Point Park, an area north of Dubuque. The park features many trails along the river. You will also find a small dam and lock that links to the O'Leary Lake on the border with Wisconsin.

The park includes a bandshell where public concerts take place during the summer season. There's also a massive statue of an eagle overlooking the park entrance.

Best Time to Visit:
It is easier to access the park from May to October during its official season. The park is closed to vehicles during the off-season, but pedestrian traffic is still welcome during that time.

Pass/Permit/Fees:
Pedestrians can enter the park for free, but it costs $1 for vehicles or $5 for buses.

Closest City or Town:
Dubuque

Physical Address:
2601 Shiras Ave, Dubuque, IA 52001

GPS Coordinates:
42.53720° N, 90.65264° W

Did You Know?
Much of the park was built during the 1930s as part of the Works Progress Administration.

Effigy Mounds National Monument

The northeastern Iowa town of Harpers Ferry is home to the Effigy Mounds National Monument. This monument houses about 200 prehistoric mounds built by local natives. Many of the mounds here were shaped to look like animals, chosen to represent various seasonal or celestial events. The Big Bear Mound is the largest of the mounds, as it is about 42 meters in size between its two ends.

Some of the mounds are in the Driftless Area, a region that did not experience glaciation during the past ice age. The area features many small islands and caves that remain intact.

Best Time to Visit:
Visit during the spring, as the leaf cover will not be as dense.

Pass/Permit/Fees:
The monument is free to visit.

Closest City or Town:
Dubuque

Physical Address:
151 IA-76, Harpers Ferry, IA 52146

GPS Coordinates:
43.08972° N, 91.210073° W

Did You Know?
The Effigy Mounds were honored on a United States quarter in 2017 as part of the *America the Beautiful* quarters series.

Fenelon Place Elevator

The Fenelon Place Elevator is a unique commuter rail train in Dubuque that travels 296 feet to the top of a hill nearly 200 feet upward. The elevator is one of the world's steepest rail lines. The elevator was built in the 1880s as a site for observation. People can see views of the Mississippi River and parts of Illinois and Wisconsin. The top spot features a small observation tower that you can reach to see more of the local area. The cable cars are also designed so that the two separate cars that go up and down will meet each other at the same point, producing power that counterbalances the two cars.

Best Time to Visit:
The elevator is open from April to November.

Pass/Permit/Fees:
A round-trip ticket on the elevator is $4 for adults and $2 for children. Bicycle riders cost $3 each way. This venue is a cash-only spot.

Closest City or Town:
Dubuque

Physical Address:
512 Fenelon Pl, Dubuque, IA 52001

GPS Coordinates:
42.49736° N, 90.66935° W

Did You Know?
The design of the elevator was heavily inspired by one-car cables in the Alps and the streetcars featured during the 1893 Columbian Exposition in Chicago.

Grand Harbor Resort and Waterpark

You will find the Grand Harbor Resort and Waterpark north of the Dubuque Harbor in downtown. The resort features an indoor waterpark with about 25,000 square feet of room for activities.

The park contains multiple water slides, pools, fountains, and other features for people to enjoy. There's also a restaurant at the park with a bar for adults. This park is one part of an extended resort that also features a few high-end restaurants and a spa.

Best Time to Visit:
The park is open throughout the year, but the longest hours are during the summer season.

Pass/Permit/Fees:
It costs $18 for adults and $14 for children to visit the waterpark on weekdays. The park is reserved for resort guests only during the weekends.

Closest City or Town:
Dubuque

Physical Address:
350 Bell St, Dubuque, IA 52001

GPS Coordinates:
42.49735° N, 90.65661° W

Did You Know?
Some of the spots around the resort offer views of the nearby Dubuque Railroad Bridge that leads across the river into Illinois.

Julien Dubuque Monument

The Julien Dubuque Monument overlooks the Mississippi River near the town where the founder of the city of Dubuque started mining the land for lead. The monument is a castle-inspired Late Gothic Revival structure built in 1897. It overlooks the city of Dubuque and the Mines of Spain property.

The center of the monument features the final resting space of Dubuque. The design includes limestone materials harvested from a nearby quarry.

Best Time to Visit:
You can visit the monument during the spring when there is more light outside, and the conditions are more pleasant.

Pass/Permit/Fees:
The monument is free to visit.

Closest City or Town:
Dubuque

Physical Address:
1810 Monument Dr, Dubuque, IA 52003

GPS Coordinates:
42.46905° N, 90.64822° W

Did You Know?
The castle-like design of the monument is a characteristic of Late Gothic Revival structures. You'll notice a massive look to the monument while the windows are narrow and slim.

Mathias Ham House

The Mathias Ham House is an 1856 Late Victorian house built for a local lead miner. The house features a unique design reflective of Iowa during the Antebellum era. You can tour the house and visit its museum to learn about life during that time. The property contains many furnishings from the United States and Europe during the nineteenth century.

The Mathias Ham House is on a lot that also includes a one-room schoolhouse and a re-created mine shaft. There's also a double log cabin on the site that was built in 1833 and is believed to be the state's oldest building.

Best Time to Visit:
You can visit the house throughout the year, although the winter is a very picturesque time to see it.

Pass/Permit/Fees:
Admission is $7.50 for adults and $4 for children.

Closest City or Town:
Dubuque

Physical Address:
2241 Lincoln Ave, Dubuque, IA 52001

GPS Coordinates:
42.53192° N, 90.65062° W

Did You Know?
The home was designed by John F. Rague, who also designed the original state capitol building in Iowa City.

Mines of Spain Recreation Area

You will find about 1,400 acres of land at the Mines of Spain Recreation Area in Dubuque. Its center is near the Granger Creek and Catfish Creek, leading toward the Mississippi River. There are 21 miles of hiking trails around the area. Of these, 6 miles of trails are open for cross-country skiing during the winter. Many of the trails will bring you across native prairie lands and limestone bluffs. The area also features a few spots for wildlife viewing, including somewhere you can see bald eagles and other birds of prey during the migratory season.

Best Time to Visit:
Visit during the fall, as many migratory birds will make their way through the area during that season.

Pass/Permit/Fees:
You can visit the area for free, although donations are recommended.

Closest City or Town:
Dubuque

Physical Address:
10426 Mines of Spain Rd, Dubuque, IA 52003

GPS Coordinates:
42.45696° N, 90.62952° W

Did You Know?
The Mines of Spain get their name from the Governor of New Spain. The governor granted the area for mining activities in 1796.

National Mississippi River Museum and Aquarium

You will find the National Mississippi River Museum and Aquarium on the shore of the river in Dubuque. This Smithsonian-affiliated museum highlights the uniqueness of the Mississippi River, offering exhibits on its various wildlife and plants as well as a look at river travel. The museum features a train depot and an old-time blacksmithing shop. You'll also find the *William M. Black,* a steam-propelled dredge ship.

Best Time to Visit:
The museum and aquarium are open throughout the year, but there are some special exhibits during certain times.

Pass/Permit/Fees:
Admission is $19.95 for adults and $14.95 for children. The all-access pass offers both admission and access to a film for $5 extra per person. It also costs $10 to get access to the stingray-feeding section.

Closest City or Town:
Dubuque

Physical Address:
350 E 3rd St, Dubuque, IA 52001

GPS Coordinates:
42.49758° N, 90.66134° W

Did You Know?
The museum also houses the National Rivers Hall of Fame, a site devoted to people who made their living on rivers.

Park Farm Winery

The Park Farm Winery in Durango is a family-owned property featuring a rolling vineyard that produces the grapes for the winery's many products. The winery contains a dining space where you can enjoy a glass of wine and watch the sunset near the Mississippi River. The winery also has a wood-fired oven so that you can enjoy a pizza with your wine. The winery staff can provide recommendations for what pizzas go well with whatever wines you order. The wine selection at the Park Farm Winery includes various red, white, and fruit wines. Some of the wines work well as spritzers with other drinks.

Best Time to Visit:
The winery is open throughout the year, although the summer is the best time to visit. Try to arrive close to sunset if possible.

Pass/Permit/Fees:
The prices for the wines and food here will vary by option—many of the bottles of wine cost from $20 to $30.

Closest City or Town:
Dubuque

Physical Address:
15159 Thielen Rd, Durango, IA 52039

GPS Coordinates:
42.51450° N, 90.91439° W

Did You Know?
You can bring a picnic lunch to the winery if you are interested.

Pikes Peak State Park

Pikes Peak in Colorado isn't the only famous summit in the country that's named after Zebulon Pike. Pikes Peak in northeastern Iowa is a 500-foot bluff that looks over the Mississippi and Wisconsin rivers.

You can visit Pikes Peak in Iowa while at the Pikes Peak State Park. You will also find Bear Mound, an old effigy built by Native Americans. There is a separate 4-mile trail that leads to views of the nearby town of McGregor. The park also features a playground for kids to enjoy.

Best Time to Visit:
The summer is the best time to visit, as you are less likely to see lots of fog building up around the park.

Pass/Permit/Fees:
The park is free to visit.

Closest City or Town:
Dubuque

Physical Address:
32264 Pikes Peak Rd, McGregor, IA 52157

GPS Coordinates:
42.99610° N, 91.16599° W

Did You Know?
Most of the land around the park has not been cleared for developmental purposes. Many of the spots look the same as they did prior to white settlement in the area.

Point Ann Trail

You will find beautiful views of McGregor Lake and the Mississippi River from Point Ann Trail in the northeastern part of the state. The trail is a 0.6-mile path for hiking and walking.

The Point Ann Trail brings you through the back end of Pikes Peak State Park. You will find many sites for birding in addition to the wild raspberries and other plants along the path.

Best Time to Visit:
The spring and fall seasons are great times to visit, as they are popular times for mushroom hunting. You will find many mushrooms growing and blooming around the trail.

Pass/Permit/Fees:
You can visit the trail for free.

Closest City or Town:
Dubuque

Physical Address:
32264 Pikes Peak Rd, McGregor, IA 52157

GPS Coordinates:
42,99770° N, 91.16612° W

Did You Know?
The trail is near a small shack in southwestern McGregor, where the Ringling family lived in the 1860s. The family formed the famous Ringling Brothers Circus while living here.

Shot Tower

You will find the Shot Tower in Dubuque on the Mississippi River near the city's Riverwalk. The tower is about 120 feet high and was built in 1856. The shot tower helped produce lead shot for firearms. The tall design of the shot tower comes from a grate at the top that would collect molten lead. The droplets from that grate would fall and create a solid sphere shape as they landed in the water, cooling off the material and producing the shot needed for firearms. The tower was also used as a watchtower for a local lumber company.

Best Time to Visit:
You can visit at any time, although getting to the top of the tower is dependent on the time of year.

Pass/Permit/Fees:
You can visit the outside for free. Tours are not typically available.

Closest City or Town:
Dubuque

Physical Address:
E Commercial St, Dubuque, IA 52001

GPS Coordinates:
42.50128° N, 90.65407° W

Did You Know?
The shot tower in Dubuque is one of the last remaining shot towers of its kind that is still standing. Most of these buildings were constructed in the mid-to-late nineteenth century.

Sky Tours at YMCA Union Park Camp

You can go ziplining over Dubuque at the YMCA Union Park Camp. The Sky Tours attraction at the camp features nine lines that you can enjoy over a two-hour trip. These lines go up to 1,000 feet in length, and the maximum height is about 75 feet. You'll see the ruins of Union Park from up in the sky. Union Park was a formal garden and entertainment site. You can find many of the different footprints for some of the venue's sites from atop the lines. One of the lines will lead you towards a spot where Cooper's hawks can be found. You can see a vast nest for the hawks and hear their distinctive calls when you get near the area.

Best Time to Visit:
Tours are open throughout the year, although the spring and summer seasons are the best times to visit.

Pass/Permit/Fees:
It costs $74 per person to go on a ziplining tour. Local YMCA members receive a discounted price of $69.

Closest City or Town:
Dubuque

Physical Address:
11764 John F Kennedy Rd, Dubuque, IA 52001

GPS Coordinates:
42.53931° N, 90.71584° W

Did You Know?
The YMCA and Boy Scouts have owned this land since 1946.

Stone Cliff Winery

The Stone Cliff Winery is inside a historic building near the Dubuque Railroad Bridge on the Mississippi River. The winery features a tasting room where you can try many of the different wines grown in the winery's rural vineyards. This location features wines of all sorts for people to try, including an apple cranberry wine and a cabernet sauvignon. The place also has a lunch menu, and you can reserve a spot at the winery's mystery dinner theater. Everything here is inside the Star Brewery Building, an 1898 building that has been heavily renovated over the years.

Best Time to Visit:
The winery is open throughout the year, although some of the offerings are seasonal.

Pass/Permit/Fees:
You can visit the tasting room for $10. Wines and other products are also available for sale.

Closest City or Town:
Dubuque

Physical Address:
600 Star Brewery Drive, Dubuque, IA 52001

GPS Coordinates:
42.49966° N, 90.65385° W

Did You Know?
The winery sells personalized wine bottles. You can request any message on one of these bottles.

Storybook Hill Children's Zoo

The Storybook Hill Children's Zoo is designed for children. It teaches them about some of the most common animals found at a farm. Kids can see and learn about cows, rabbits, pigs, and many other animals. Visitors can hear about how these animals are cared for, why they are valuable, and how they can grow from small newborns to larger adults.

The zoo features a play area for the kids to enjoy. Everything is situated around various beautiful green spaces that provide a fun environment for families.

Best Time to Visit:
The zoo is open from May to Labor Day each year.

Pass/Permit/Fees:
The zoo is free to enter.

Closest City or Town:
Dubuque

Physical Address:
12201 N Cascade Rd, Dubuque, IA 52003

GPS Coordinates:
42.46781° N, 90.72868° W

Did You Know?
The zoo features a few pavilions you can rent for birthday parties and other special family occasions.

Sundown Mountain

You'll find many places for skiing and snowboarding during the winter season at Sundown Mountain outside Dubuque. The mountain resort features 21 ski runs of all levels. You'll also find two terrain parks for freestyle skiing here. The mountain has a vertical drop of about 475 feet and features four lifts. The mountain has lights all around to help you see through even the toughest conditions. You can also choose different routes of varying difficulty levels based on your skiing experience. The mountain offers skiing lessons to interested parties, and there is a kids' play area for the little ones.

Best Time to Visit:
The mountain is open from November to February.

Pass/Permit/Fees:
A lift ticket is available for as little as $19, although the prices will vary based on the day of the week or time of the year.

Closest City or Town:
Dubuque

Physical Address:
16991 Asbury Rd. Dubuque, IA

GPS Coordinates:
42.51700° N, 90.81859° W

Did You Know?
This mountain resort hosts some statewide skiing competitions every year, although the calendar for what the resort will host will vary.

Field of Dreams Movie Site

The Field of Dreams Movie Site is a must-see spot for baseball and film fans. The site in the Dubuque County town of Dyersville is home to a baseball field used in the 1989 film *Field of Dreams*.

There is also a farmhouse that was prominently highlighted in the film and a baseball diamond used for many of the scenes in the movie. You'll find a wooden bench in the area with the famed inscription "Ray Loves Annie" etched on its body. You can tour the home on the movie site and learn about its use in the film. The field is also open for people wanting to play catch, and it's available for rentals.

Best Time to Visit:
The movie site is open throughout the year, although it is more popular during the baseball season.

Pass/Permit/Fees:
Tours of the site are $20 for adults and $12 for children.

Closest City or Town:
Dyersville

Physical Address:
28995 Lansing Rd, Dyersville, IA 52040

GPS Coordinates:
42.49783° N, 91.05429° W

Did You Know?
The movie site hosted a Major League Baseball game between the Chicago White Sox and New York Yankees in August 2021.

American Gothic House

The Wapello County town of Eldon features the house that artist Grant Wood used as the backdrop of his iconic 1930 painting *American Gothic*. This 1882 structure is known as "the American Gothic House," but its official name is the Dibble House, after the property's first owner. The design of the home was used in Wood's painting behind a farmer with a pitchfork next to a woman that some claim to be his wife and some his daughter. While you can't go inside the house itself, you can visit the nearby center to learn all about the painting. The center features various exhibits about the painting and Wood's work. There's also a sidewalk that leads to the front of the house for pictures. You can even borrow a costume and pitchfork for a photo.

Best Time to Visit:
You can visit the house from Wednesday through Sunday.

Pass/Permit/Fees:
The house and center are open for free.

Closest City or Town:
Eldon

Physical Address:
300 American Gothic St, Eldon, IA 52554

GPS Coordinates:
40.92159° N, 92.21385° W

Did You Know?
Grant Wood chose this house in Eldon as the backdrop for his painting because he found the design to be "cardboardy" and easy to paint.

Elkader Whitewater Park

Go paddling down the Turkey River at the Elkader Whitewater Park. This park in northeastern Iowa features a small trail for tubing, kayaking, and fishing. The whitewater park was built in 2013 and features a 22-foot fast-flowing wave called the Gobbler Wave that allows people to test their paddling skills.

The water flows slowly as you progress, with some spots near the end of the path being gentle enough for fish to swim and for people to enjoy fishing. The park is a portion of the Elkader City Park. The venue features multiple athletic courts and a small disc golf course.

Best Time to Visit:
The area is most active during the summer months.

Pass/Permit/Fees:
You can visit the park for free, but you will have to pay money to rent a kayak or other piece of water equipment.

Closest City or Town:
Elkader

Physical Address:
211 S Main St, Elkader, IA 52043

GPS Coordinates:
42.85338° N, 91.40283° W

Did You Know?
Part of the park is near the Keystone Bridge that goes over the river. The bridge is notable for its classic stone build.

Maharishi Vedic City

You will find Maharishi Vedic City north of Fairfield in Jefferson County. The city is relatively new, as it was incorporated in 2001. The 1-square-mile city is designed based on the principles of Maharishi Sthapatya Veda.

The Vedic style of architecture and design in the city is based on general values focusing on social and religious traditions. All rooms in the properties are arranged based on the sun's movements, and the entrances face due east. The buildings also feature a silent core in the middle, golden roof fixtures, and a perimeter fence. You'll also find an outdoor observatory with ten astronomical tools. These are aligned based on the stars' movements and are believed to create balance in the mind.

Best Time to Visit:
The city is open to visit throughout the year.

Pass/Permit/Fees:
You can visit the city for free.

Closest City or Town:
Fairfield

Physical Address:
1750 Maharishi Center Ave, Fairfield, IA 52556

GPS Coordinates:
41.05369° N, 92.00649° W

Did You Know?
Sanskrit is considered the preferred language in the city, although English is more commonly used here.

Lacey Keosauqua State Park

The Lacey Keosauqua State Park is the state's largest, with about 1,650 acres at the southeastern end near the Des Moines River.

The park features a 3-mile trail surrounding the Des Moines River. You will also find some Native American burial mounds near the river around the Woodland Culture overlook. There is also a 30-acre lake at the park where you can go boating with an electric motor vessel.

Best Time to Visit:
The spring is the best time to visit, as it is great for birdwatching.

Pass/Permit/Fees:
You can visit the park for free, but it may cost extra to rent a campsite or reserve a spot on the boat deck.

Closest City or Town:
Fort Madison

Physical Address:
22895 Lacey Trail, Keosauqua, IA 52565

GPS Coordinates:
40.71281° N, 91.98137° W

Did You Know?
The park's name comes from the Sauk name for the Des Moines River, which loosely translates to "bend in the river."

Matchstick Marvels

The Matchstick Marvels museum in Gladbrook features various art models created out of matchsticks. The museum houses models designed by local resident Pat Acton, who has been building these models since the 1970s. The models are unpainted and glued one at a time. You will find dozens of works at the museum, including ones for the United States Capitol and the Notre Dame Cathedral. There are also a few pop culture-inspired models here, including one of Hogwarts from the Harry Potter series that is made of nearly 600,000 sticks. Some of these models have appeared in various art exhibits throughout the world, including a model of the International Space Station that was once displayed at the NASA Houston Space Center.

Best Time to Visit:
The museum is open between April and November.

Pass/Permit/Fees:
Admission is $5 for adults and $3 for children.

Closest City or Town:
Gladbrook

Physical Address:
319 2nd St, Gladbrook, IA 50635

GPS Coordinates:
42.18857° N, 92.71544° W

Did You Know?
Acton does not paint any of his works because he feels the paint will cover up the details. One model of a P-51 Mustang was painted, but he wishes he hadn't done so.

Devonian Fossil Gorge

The Devonian Fossil Gorge is north of Iowa City. The site features a prehistoric ocean floor dating back about 375 million years.

The gorge contains many heavily fossilized land spaces in lime. The surface reveals many imprinted sites with different tracks and prints, highlighting the wildlife that lived here in prehistoric times.

The gorge is west of Coralville Lake, near the Iowa River. It is located near a small dam on the Iowa River that helps keep the ocean floor from flooding.

Best Time to Visit:
Visit during the daytime hours to get the best possible views of some of the remnants around the area.

Pass/Permit/Fees:
You can enter the gorge for free.

Closest City or Town:
Iowa City

Physical Address:
2850 Prairie Du Chien Rd NE, Iowa City, 52240

GPS Coordinates:
41.72243° N, 91.53233° W

Did You Know?
Much of the gorge wasn't revealed until 1993, when heavy rainfall caused silt and sand to erode over it.

Future Birthplace of James T. Kirk

The town of Riverside is home to the future birthplace of Captain James T. Kirk, the main character of the classic television series *Star Trek*. Series creator Gene Roddenberry once said that Kirk was from Iowa. A few Star Trek–related books suggest that Kirk's birthplace is in Riverside, thus leading to the town staking its claim as his birthplace. The city features a marker listing where he will be born on March 22, 2228. The city also houses the Voyage Home Riverside History Center, a venue that features many exhibits dedicated to the history of the Star Trek franchise. The museum has a section devoted to a visit in 2004 from the original Captain Kirk, William Shatner.

Best Time to Visit:
The site is very popular around March 22.

Pass/Permit/Fees:
You can visit the area for free.

Closest City or Town:
Iowa City

Physical Address:
60 Greene St, Riverside, IA 52327

GPS Coordinates:
41.48062° N, 91.58049° W

Did You Know?
The March 22 birthdate has never been officially confirmed in any *Star Trek* books, shows, or films, but the year 2228 has been confirmed. March 22 is William Shatner's birthday.

Iowa City

Iowa City is a memorable town in Johnson County that is worth visiting. It's home to the University of Iowa and the Old Capitol Building in the middle of the university campus. Iowa City is known for many historic sites, including the Moffitt cottages. The Ned Ashton House is also a prominent meeting space in Iowa City that hosts various parties and events each year. The city also has a pedestrian mall called City Plaza, which is home to many local businesses and dining spots, as well as the Iowa City Public Library.

Best Time to Visit:
The city hosts various concerts and other programs in the summer during its *Summer of the Arts* series.

Pass/Permit/Fees:
Admission for different sites around Iowa City will vary by venue.

Closest City or Town:
Iowa City

Physical Address:
213 N Clinton St, Iowa City, IA 52245

GPS Coordinates:
41.66672° N, 91.53567° W

Did You Know?
Kinnick Stadium on the University of Iowa campus is home to the school's football team. It is one of the largest athletic stadiums in the country, with a maximum capacity of about 70,000 people.

Kinnick Stadium

Kinnick Stadium is on the University of Iowa campus in Iowa City. The football stadium has been the home of the Iowa Hawkeyes since 1929. The stadium has room for 70,000 fans on game days. It also features a 20-foot statue of the stadium's namesake, Heisman Trophy-winning player Nile Kinnick. The University of Iowa Children's Hospital also overlooks the eastern end of the stadium. After the first quarter of each game, the fans and players will wave at the children watching the game from the hospital.

Best Time to Visit:
Kinnick Stadium hosts many college football events throughout the year. Check with the school to see when the Hawkeyes are playing.

Pass/Permit/Fees:
Tours are available, although the cost will vary throughout the year.

Closest City or Town:
Iowa City

Physical Address:
825 Stadium Dr, Iowa City, IA 52240

GPS Coordinates:
41.65788° N, 91.54745° W

Did You Know?
The visitor locker room has a distinct coating of pink paint. Former coach John Hayden Fry insisted on the paint color in that room.

The Black Angel of Oakland Cemetery

The Oakland Cemetery in Iowa City has served the community since 1843. It is the final resting space of Governor Samuel Kirkwood, artist Mauricio Lasansky, and television news reporter Bobbie Battista. The most noteworthy feature of the cemetery is the *Black Angel* statue. The 1913 statue by Mario Korbel was designed as part of a memorial to someone from the present-day Czech Republic. The statue has a black color and features an angel with its wings spread outward. The angel is believed to be a bad omen to many people. Some argue that if someone touches the statue, that person will die unless they are a virgin. There's also a belief that if a pregnant woman walks under the statue, she will miscarry.

Best Time to Visit:
The cemetery and statue are open to visit throughout the year.

Pass/Permit/Fees:
You can visit the area for free.

Closest City or Town:
Iowa City

Physical Address:
704 Reno St, Iowa City, IA 52245

GPS Coordinates:
41.67036° N, 91.51834° W

Did You Know?
Many people often come to the statue on Halloween to test the superstitions surrounding it.

Swinging Bridge

Assembly Park in Iowa Falls is home to the Swinging Bridge, one of the most interesting sites in the state. The current bridge has stood since 1989, although the original one was built in 1897.

The bridge goes over the Iowa River towards Rocksylvania Avenue. You'll notice when crossing the bridge that it does swing a bit as you walk over the space. The design features multiple cables around the sides to ensure its stability.

You'll be rewarded with outstanding views of nearby Iowa Falls while you're on the bridge. You'll also find the Swinging Bridge Cottage on the other side of the river.

Best Time to Visit:
Visit during the winter, as you will find beautiful views of the city when it is covered in snow.

Pass/Permit/Fees:
You can get on the bridge for free.

Closest City or Town:
Iowa Falls

Physical Address:
Rocksylvania Ave, Iowa Falls, IA 50126

GPS Coordinates:
42.52229° N, 93.27074° W

Did You Know?
The bridge has been rebuilt four times since it was first created in 1897.

Lake Sugema

Lake Sugema is at the southeastern end of the state in Van Buren County, south of Des Moines River.

Lake Sugema offers various fishing jetties, although you can also take a boat to the middle of the lake if you prefer. Visitors are required to release any 12- to 18-inch black bass fish, they find here.

Most of the fishing and recreational activities are in the central part of the lake. You'll find open spaces for picnics, camping spots, hiking trails, and even a fish-cleaning station on site.

Best Time to Visit:
The water conditions are gentle during the spring season.

Pass/Permit/Fees:
Admission is free, but a permit is necessary for fishing.

Closest City or Town:
Keosauqua

Physical Address:
19640 Jersey Ave, Keosauqua, IA

GPS Coordinates:
40.68320° N, 91.99506° W

Did You Know?
Much of the lake is surrounded by small farm ponds and farming space that is consistently rotated. These efforts reduce the risk of siltation, ensuring the water remains stable and clean for everyone to enjoy.

National Sprint Car Hall of Fame

You will find the National Sprint Car Hall of Fame near the northeastern end of the Knoxville Raceway in the Marion County town of Knoxville. The hall highlights the history of sprint car racing and honors the greatest racers in the field. You'll see 25 sprint cars from the history of the sport that has been refurbished and cleaned for display. These include many sprint cars that competed in the World of Outlaws series. These sprint cars are used on short oval or circular tracks and feature a high power-to-weight ratio similar to what Formula One cars use.

Best Time to Visit:
The museum is popular on race nights, which can vary throughout the year.

Pass/Permit/Fees:
Admission is $5 for adults and $4 for seniors.

Closest City or Town:
Knoxville

Physical Address:
1 Sprint Capital Place, Knoxville, IA 50138

GPS Coordinates:
41.32820° N, 93.11014° W

Did You Know?
Sprint car racing has long been the first stop for professional auto racers. Many IndyCar and NASCAR drivers started driving sprint cars before making their way to the top auto-racing groups.

Black Hawk Lake

Black Hawk Lake is in northwestern Iowa, midway between Des Moines and Sioux City. This lake in Sac County is a small tributary of the nearby North Raccoon River.

You'll find many boating docks along the perimeter of the lake, with most to the south. The docks will lead you to nearly 900 acres of water with a maximum depth of about 15 feet. Some of the fish you can catch include bluegill, walleye, yellow perch, crappie, and catfish.

Best Time to Visit:
The spring and summer are good times to visit, as the water is a little warmer during those seasons. You'll have an easier time finding fish during that point.

Pass/Permit/Fees:
Access is free, but a fishing license in Iowa is necessary.

Closest City or Town:
Lake View

Physical Address:
228 S Blossom St, Lake View, IA 51450

GPS Coordinates:
42.29520° N, 95.01920° W

Did You Know?
The lake is named for Chief Black Hawk, the leader of the Sauk tribe.

Nine Eagles State Park

Nine Eagles State Park is located near the south-central part of Iowa, next to the Missouri border. The park features 1,100 acres of land with plenty of camping sites and activities throughout the area.

This park has 6 miles of equestrian trails and nine more miles for hiking. There are many native prairie spots throughout these trails. You'll find a fishing jetty and a boating dock as well as a fish-cleaning station.

Best Time to Visit:
You'll have an easier time finding fish here during the spring season. The weather will also be more tolerable at that point in the year.

Pass/Permit/Fees:
Admission is free, but the cost will vary for each service, such as renting a campsite or accessing the dock with your boat.

Closest City or Town:
Leon

Physical Address:
23678 Dale Miller Rd, Davis City, IA 50065

GPS Coordinates:
40.58877° N, 93.75432° W

Did You Know?
The park caters to all campers and offers many different sites. There's a cabin that families can rent and a campsite exclusively open to youth groups.

High Trestle Trail Bridge

The town of Madrid in Boone County features one of the world's tallest foot-traffic bridges. The High Trestle Trail Bridge is about 13 stories high over the Des Moines River to the west of Madrid. The bridge is about half a mile long and features beautiful views of the local valley.

You'll find the remnants of some mining shafts around the bridge area. Much of the bridge features an architectural design with a mine-inspired build.

The trail bridge leads to the Raccoon River Valley Trail past Woodward. The bridge is a small part of a trail that travels about 25 miles.

Best Time to Visit:
The bridge is great to visit during the winter if you're looking for a unique snow scene in Iowa.

Pass/Permit/Fees:
You can visit the bridge for free.

Closest City or Town:
Madrid

Physical Address:
2335 Qf Ln, Madrid, IA 50156

GPS Coordinates:
41.87321° N, 93.85032° W

Did You Know?
The bridge was originally designed for railroad traffic, but it was converted into a pedestrian bridge a few years later.

Manchester Whitewater Park

You can take a spin at Manchester Whitewater Park if you want to learn how to paddle a boat on the rapids. This park features a gentle 800-foot path with a few drops. You'll find six 18-inch drops throughout the rapids trail, testing your ability to keep your vessel in check. This location is open for kayaking and tubing. The gradual slope on the trail allows the river to naturally flow in one direction, producing a good path for paddling. The slope also allows fish to move downstream without obstructions.

Best Time to Visit:
The park is open throughout the year, although the spring and summer are the best for visiting.

Pass/Permit/Fees:
Everything at the park is free, thanks to the park's many donors and patrons. A helmet is required for access since there are plenty of rocks sticking out of the water.

Closest City or Town:
Manchester

Physical Address:
300 W Main St, Manchester, IA 52057

GPS Coordinates:
42.48430° N, 91.46061° W

Did You Know?
Part of the whitewater path goes through the Riverfront Park in downtown Manchester. You can find the park and its gazebo near the Marion Street Bridge.

Maquoketa Caves State Park

The Maquoketa Caves State Park has more caves than any other state park in Iowa. The caves in Jackson County are part of the Driftless Area. They have been explored by many people since at least the mid-nineteenth century and continue to offer amazing views.

You will find 13 caves throughout the park, including the Dancehall Cave, with nearly 1,000 feet of space. The park also offers an interpretive center that highlights the geology of the area. Other features at the park include about 6 miles of hiking trails and dozens of campsites.

Best Time to Visit:
The summer is a good time to visit, as the caves offer plenty of cool air.

Pass/Permit/Fees:
The park is free to enter, but there is a charge for camp reservations.

Closest City or Town:
Maquoketa

Physical Address:
9688 Caves Rd, Maquoketa, IA 52060

GPS Coordinates:
42.12079° N, 90.76580° W

Did You Know?
Some Native American artifacts have been discovered around the caves over the years, revealing their presence in the Raccoon Creek valleys in the past.

Big Treehouse

The Big Treehouse in the Marshall County town of Marshalltown was first built in 1983, and it continues to grow today. The treehouse is about 5,000 square feet in size and has 12 levels. It is part of the Shady Oaks Campground.

The treehouse features a running water system, a dedicated electric system, and multiple porch swings. You'll find a 50-foot flower box and models of some of the local bridges, one of which you can cross. There's also a 60-step spiral staircase that leads through much of the treehouse, although you'll need a ladder to reach the final level.

Best Time to Visit:
The treehouse is open mostly during the spring and summer seasons.

Pass/Permit/Fees:
The cost to visit will vary by season. You can only visit the Big Treehouse by appointment.

Closest City or Town:
Marshalltown

Physical Address:
2370 Shady Oaks Rd, Marshalltown, IA 50158

GPS Coordinates:
42.01183° N, 92.85360° W

Did You Know?
The treehouse only had two floors when it first opened in 1983.

Beeds Lake State Park

The Beeds Lake State Park is located in northern Iowa, south of Mason City. This park features about 300 acres of land, about a third of which is occupied by a reservoir. You'll find many fishing and hiking sites throughout the park. The area also includes a small man-made waterfall.

The park offers an extensive walking trail that extends nearly 2 miles around the lake. Part of the trail goes across a bridge that heads over the western end. There's also a boating ramp on the southern end of the park for fun water activities.

Best Time to Visit:
Visit during the summer, as the conditions here are a little cooler than they are in other parts of the state.

Pass/Permit/Fees:
It is free to visit the park, although it may cost extra to reserve a camping site.

Closest City or Town:
Mason City

Physical Address:
1422 165th St, Hampton, IA 50441

GPS Coordinates:
42.76909° N, 93.24290° W

Did You Know?
Much of the park was built by the Civilian Conservation Corps.

Willow Creek Waterfall

The peaceful scene of Willow Creek Waterfall in Mason City is one of the area's most popular natural sites. The waterfall is in the eastern part of Mason City off of the East State Bridge near the Rock Crest historical district.

The waterfall cascades down various limestone formations. You'll notice multiple small gaps in the middle of the waterfall, adding slight accents.

The waterfall is near the southern end of the East Park region of Mason City. You'll also find a few trails for hiking and walking, plus a small playground for kids.

Best Time to Visit:
The spring season is the most temperate time to visit.

Pass/Permit/Fees:
You can visit the area for free.

Closest City or Town:
Mason City

Physical Address:
E. State Street, Mason City, IA 50401

GPS Coordinates:
43.15235° N, 93.18600° W

Did You Know?
The East Park region is one of Mason City's most popular recreational sites. You'll find an aquatic center, a bandshell, and a softball complex in the area.

DeSoto Lake

DeSoto Lake is a small channel formed off the Missouri River. This lake is part of the border between Iowa and Nebraska and creates a bend that goes north from the Missouri River.

The area features snow geese, plovers, herons, and many other birds to spot. You'll also find many fish here, including walleye, white and yellow bass, and bluegill.

Best Time to Visit:
The fall season is great, as you'll find many migrating birds during that time.

Pass/Permit/Fees:
You will require a fishing license if you wish to fish in the lake. You may require a license in either Iowa or Nebraska depending on where on the lake you plan to fish.

Closest City or Town:
Missouri Valley

Physical Address:
1434 316th Ln, Missouri Valley, IA 51555

GPS Coordinates:
41.54130° N, 96.03114° W

Did You Know?
The De Soto Lake was formed in the 1950s after the Army Corps of Engineers created a channel that helped bypass the bend. The lake was part of the Missouri River before that construction project.

Coralville Lake

Coralville Lake is in between Iowa City and Cedar Rapids in Johnson County. The lake is produced by a 1950s dam from the nearby Iowa River.

Coralville Lake features seven trails with nearly 30 miles of space around the area. The lake includes three marinas for boating and a few swimming beaches in the area. You can also play on one of the two disc golf courses at the lake.

Best Time to Visit:
The spring is an ideal time to visit, especially when new trees and plants are beginning to grow.

Pass/Permit/Fees:
You can visit for free, but it costs extra to rent disc golf equipment or access one of the boating docks.

Closest City or Town:
North Liberty

Physical Address:
3369 Sandy Beach Rd NE, Solon, IA 52333

GPS Coordinates:
41.81630° N, 91.59979° W

Did You Know?
The Devonian Fossil Gorge was revealed in the area following a then-record crest of the lake during the Great Flood of 1993. The lake crested further in the 2008 Midwest Floods.

Lake Macbride State Park

You'll find Lake Macbride State Park midway between Cedar Rapids and Iowa City near Lake Macbride, the Iowa River, and Coralville Lake. The park offers many nature trails that lead to habitats featuring native Iowan birds like the American goldfinch, woodpecker, finch, and American robin. The lake features about 7 miles of trails for hiking. These trails are also open for cross-country skiing and snowmobiling during the winter season. The lake also has four shelters and many camping sites that you can reserve throughout the year. There are both electric and non-electric campsites.

Best Time to Visit:
The spring is a good time to visit when the conditions are temperate.

Pass/Permit/Fees:
You can enter the park for free, but it costs extra to reserve a boat or equipment.

Closest City or Town:
North Liberty

Physical Address:
3525 Hwy 382 NE, Solon, IA 52333

GPS Coordinates:
41.80464° N, 91.57108° W

Did You Know?
The park is named for Thomas Macbride, one of the leaders of conservation efforts in Iowa.

Big Spirit Lake

Big Spirit Lake is part of the Iowa Great Lakes at the northern end of the state. This body of water in Dickinson County is the largest natural lake in Iowa, with a surface area of about 5,700 acres.

Big Spirit Lake is an exciting place for fishing where you can find freshwater drum, largemouth and smallmouth bass, and northern pike. Kiteboarding is also available throughout the area.

Best Time to Visit:
Visit during the morning, as the temperatures aren't as harsh then. You may also find more fish near the surface if you go fishing early.

Pass/Permit/Fees:
You can visit for free, but you must have an Iowa license to fish.

Closest City or Town:
Orleans

Physical Address:
12320 240th Ave, Spirit Lake, IA 51360

GPS Coordinates:
43.47430° N, 95.12549° W

Did You Know?
Much of the lake is inside a glacial pothole that was formed nearly 13,000 years ago during the last ice age.

Three Mile Lake

Three Mile Lake, in Union County, features a few fishing jetties, plus a boating dock at the northern end. You can go fishing for walleye, crappie, and blue catfish. The lake area features a small lodge for events, and it surrounds hundreds of acres of land that are open for hunting. You can hunt for waterfowl here, although hunting Canadian geese is prohibited. Pheasant, quail, and wild turkeys can also be found around the area.

Best Time to Visit:
The fall and winter are great times to visit, as there are plenty of migrating birds around the area during those seasons.

Pass/Permit/Fees:
It costs $17 to reserve an electric campsite for an evening or $10 for a non-electric site.

Closest City or Town:
Osceola

Physical Address:
There is a beach three miles north of US Highway 34 at Afton, IA 50830.

GPS Coordinates:
41.08168° N, 94.22142° W

Did You Know?
The extensive amount of cover and food around the lake make this area a prominent site for migrating birds. You can find hundreds to thousands of them in the area on an average day during the fall or winter.

Lake Red Rock

You can visit Lake Red Rock, northeast of Des Moines, while in Iowa. The lake is near the Des Moines River and is formed by the nearby Red River Dam. The area provides multiple opportunities for fishing, sailing, and viewing nature.

You'll find Cordova Park at the northern end of the lake and the observational Cordova Tower that provides views from about 100 feet up. You can also go boating near the Mile Long Bridge in the middle part of the lake.

Best Time to Visit:
The summer is perfect for visiting, as the longer daytime hours provide more opportunities to see the landscape from the nearby Cordova Tower.

Pass/Permit/Fees:
You can visit the lake for free.

Closest City or Town:
Pella

Physical Address:
1007 Hwy T15, Pella, IA 50219

GPS Coordinates:
41.38107° N, 92.97426° W

Did You Know?
Lake Red Rock is the largest lake in Iowa, with a surface area of about 15,000 acres. It is also 11 miles at its longest point.

Pella

The town of Pella in Marion County is one of the most distinct places to visit while in Iowa. Pella was formed by Dutch immigrants in the 1840s. This town is home to many sites that remind people of the Netherlands. You'll find a functional windmill called the Vermeer Mill in the center of the city. The windmill is nearly 130 feet high. You'll also find the Molengracht Canal in the middle of downtown Pella, reminiscent of the canals found in Amsterdam. Pella is a manufacturing hub, and the Pella Corporation is the most prominent business in the city. The company produces windows and doors for homes.

Best Time to Visit:
The town hosts the Tulip Time Festival on the first weekend of May. The festival features a Dutch garden and various other Dutch activities.

Pass/Permit/Fees:
Pella is free to visit, although it will cost to visit some sites.

Closest City or Town:
Des Moines

Physical Address:
915 Broadway St, Pella, IA 50219

GPS Coordinates:
41.40958° N, 92.91848° W

Did You Know?
Some people in Pella speak Pella Dutch, a subdialect of a form of Dutch spoken in the eastern end of the Netherlands near the Rhine.

Vermeer Windmill

The town of Pella is known for its strong Dutch influence, and the Vermeer Windmill is one of the top features in the city. The Vermeer Windmill, located in the center of the city, is a fully functioning 124-foot windmill designed to look like a traditional grain mill from the 1850s. The windmill resembles various models of other windmills you would find in the Netherlands. There's also a compact home space similar to where the miller's family would live while operating the unit. You can climb to the top of the windmill to get a great view of the city. There's also a small train set in the windmill that depicts life in the Netherlands in the 1840s.

Best Time to Visit:
The windmill is open from March to December.

Pass/Permit/Fees:
Admission to the windmill is $10 for adults and $2 for children.

Closest City or Town:
Pella

Physical Address:
714 E 1st St, Pella, IA 50219

GPS Coordinates:
41.40657° N, 92.91446° W

Did You Know?
The windmill was built in the Netherlands and disassembled for shipment to Iowa, where it was reassembled.

Avenue of Flags

The Avenue of Flags may be the most patriotic street in the country. The road in Holstein features hundreds of American flags scattered on South Kiel Street.

The flags are placed along the road in honor of military veterans who have connections to the city. There are nearly 500 American flags displayed. They're raised and lowered by local American Legion members during major holidays.

Best Time to Visit:
The avenue looks its best during the spring and summer seasons, as it is surrounded by various nearby trees.

Pass/Permit/Fees:
You can drive your way down the avenue for free.

Closest City or Town:
Sioux City

Physical Address:
South Kiel Street, Holstein, IA 51025

GPS Coordinates:
42.48285° N, 95.54331° W

Did You Know?
Each flag represents a different veteran from the local area. You'll see a listing on each pole highlighting the veteran's name, rank, branch of service, and the campaigns or other time periods in which they served.

Castles of Ida Grove

You will find a few castles throughout the Ida County town of Ida Grove. These castles are on IA-175 and feature many unique medieval designs. The castles in Ida Grove have brick-and-stone construction styles with peaks and eaves. Several of these castles feature evergreen trees that were moved from different parts of the country.

Many were built by Byron LeRoy Godberson. The industrialist was very interested in producing unique buildings that were different from everything else in Ida Grove.

Best Time to Visit:
You can visit the castles at any point in the year.

Pass/Permit/Fees:
You can see the castles for free from the outside. Some of these properties are closed to the public, so check the rules for each place before visiting.

Closest City or Town:
Sioux City

Physical Address:
203 Susan Lawrence Dr, Ida Grove, IA 51445

GPS Coordinates:
42.34675° N, 95.46999° W

Did You Know?
Godberson's most massive castle is on his private land in Lake LaJune.

Stone State Park

You will find Stone State Park in northwestern Sioux City near the Missouri River and the borders of Nebraska and South Dakota. The park is on the Big Sioux River in the Loess Hills and features a stone lodge, an old shelter spot, and about 15 miles of trails. Some of the trails around the park are open for equestrian use.

Stone State Park houses the Dorothy Pecaut Nature Center, an interpretive facility that highlights the nature of the local area. It features a simulated prairie area.

The park has some exposed bedrock surfaces. It includes shale, limestone, and other materials dating to the Cretaceous period.

Best Time to Visit:
Visit during the weekends.

Pass/Permit/Fees:
Admission to the park is free.

Closest City or Town:
Sioux City

Physical Address:
5001 Talbot Rd, Sioux City, IA 51103

GPS Coordinates:
42.54859° N, 96.46561° W

Did You Know?
You will find more than 40 species of butterfly, many of them at the nature center.

World's Largest Popcorn Ball

You'll find the World's Largest Popcorn Ball in the northwestern town of Sac City. The popcorn ball was produced in 2016 and made with about 2,300 pounds of popcorn. The ball weighs about 9,370 pounds and is 12 feet in diameter.

It is housed inside a massive tub that was used to help produce the ball. The tub is secured in a small building in part of the Sac City Museum Village, a site highlighting the history of Sac City and the prairie region of Iowa. The venue also honors Iowa's extensive agriculture history.

Best Time to Visit:
The Museum Village is open on weekends from Memorial Day to Labor Day.

Pass/Permit/Fees:
The area is free to visit.

Closest City or Town:
Sioux City

Physical Address:
1300 W Main St, Sac City, IA 50583

GPS Coordinates:
42.42328° N, 94.99951° W

Did You Know?
The state of Iowa produces at least 2 billion bushels of corn each year, which is enough to replicate the world's largest popcorn ball many times.

Backbone State Park

Backbone State Park is Iowa's oldest state park, formed in 1920. It features a bedrock ridge produced by the Maquoketa River, forming the Devil's Backbone.

The park offers about 20 miles of trails, many of these going around different trout streams. You'll find rock climbing spots around the park as well, along with dolomite limestone cliffs. The Backbone Trail features most of the park's popular climbing sites.

The streams around the park are fed by the Richmond Springs. You'll find trout, although some smaller fish may also appear at times. You can also relax on the beach at the southeastern end of the lake.

Best Time to Visit:
The summer season is the best time for fishing.

Pass/Permit/Fees:
The park offers free admission, although you must have a license for fishing.

Closest City or Town:
Strawberry Point

Physical Address:
1347 129th St, Dundee, IA 52038

GPS Coordinates:
42.60142° N, 91.53304° W

Did You Know?
The Civilian Conservation Corps has a museum at the park.

Bluedorn Science Imaginarium

The Bluedorn Science Imaginarium is a science museum in Waterloo that features many interactive exhibits for kids to enjoy. The Imaginarium has more than 90 hands-on exhibits highlighting how science plays a part in everyday life.

Among the most popular exhibits here is a hot air balloon that shows how hot air rises and can help get a balloon to take off. There's also an angular momentum machine that shows how ice skaters can move quickly and keep their balance without falling.

Best Time to Visit:
The Imaginarium is very popular during the summer season.

Pass/Permit/Fees:
Tickets are $6.

Closest City or Town:
Waterloo

Physical Address:
322 Washington St, Waterloo, IA 50701

GPS Coordinates:
42.49426° N, 92.34528° W

Did You Know?
The museum houses a section highlighting plant genomics and how they can grow in many climates and environments.

George Wyth State Park

George Wyth State Park is at the northwestern end of Waterloo. The park is a peaceful oasis from the rest of the city. It features multiple small lakes for boating and fishing along with 3 miles of paved trails and 10 miles of soft trails. This park is one of Iowa's most popular sites for birdwatching. Birding enthusiasts have found more than 200 species here. The park also has a swimming beach, a fishing pier, and various canals that link to some of the different lakes around the area.

Best Time to Visit:
Visit during the spring, as the place can become crowded during the summer.

Pass/Permit/Fees:
You can visit for free, but it may cost extra to use a boating dock or campsite. Some of the lakes here will allow electric motors but check with the park to see where you can bring your boat.

Closest City or Town:
Waterloo

Physical Address:
3659 Wyth Rd, Waterloo, IA 50703

GPS Coordinates:
42.53504° N, 92.40960° W

Did You Know?
Most of the campsites here are electric venues, but you can also find a few tent-only primitive ones.

Lost Island Waterpark

You will enjoy relaxing in the waters of the Lost Island Waterpark during the summer season while in Waterloo. Lost Island features an array of water rides, including some slides like the Lost Soul Falls and Emerald Adventure. You can also coast down the Kailahi River or swim in the Tsunami Bay wave pool.

The park features a go-karting path on its eastern end. There are also two 18-hole miniature golf courses, each featuring entertaining tropical themes.

Best Time to Visit:
Visit in June or July, as all the features in the park are open then. Some of the spots in the park are open during the offseason, but the water areas will be closed then.

Pass/Permit/Fees:
The prices for visiting will vary depending on whether you're going to the water park, the mini-golf course, or the go-kart path.

Closest City or Town:
Waterloo

Physical Address:
2225 E Shaulis Rd, Waterloo, IA 50701

GPS Coordinates:
42.44379° N, 92.31227° W

Did You Know?
The waterpark is associated with KOA, the country's top operator of privately held campgrounds.

Rensselaer Russell House Museum

The Rensselaer Russell House Museum is an 1861 property that is part of the Grout Museum District in Waterloo. The Italianate property is one of the city's first brick houses. It features Corinthian columns and a roof that slants downward from all directions.

The museum at the house features various Victorian decorations and furniture to explore. You will see what life in the area was like during the mid-nineteenth century. The designs are authentic and highlight many rustic architectural influences.

Best Time to Visit:
You can visit the house throughout the year.

Pass/Permit/Fees:
You can only visit the house if you have an appointment. The fees for entry will vary depending on the size of the party, so check with the museum first.

Closest City or Town:
Waterloo

Physical Address:
520 W 3rd St, Waterloo, IA 50701

GPS Coordinates:
42.49454° N, 92.34563° W

Did You Know?
Some of the materials used in the construction of the building had to be imported from Chicago.

Sullivan Brothers Iowa Veterans Museum

The Sullivan Brothers Iowa Veterans Museum is part of the Grout Museum District in Waterloo. The museum honors veterans from Iowa and highlights their stories from the Civil War to the present. The museum houses a veterans' memorial area and features a communication station where people can learn about how military members communicate with one another while in combat. There are also some theaters in the museum that highlight oral stories of many veterans from the state.

Best Time to Visit:
The museum often introduces new temporary exhibits, so check to see what is available before you arrive.

Pass/Permit/Fees:
Tickets are $12 for adults or $6 for children and veterans.

Closest City or Town:
Waterloo

Physical Address:
503 South St, Waterloo, IA 50701

GPS Coordinates:
42.49319° N, 92.34396° W

Did You Know?
The museum is named in honor of the five Sullivan brothers of Waterloo who died in 1942 while serving on the *USS Juneau*. The brothers were all onboard the ship when it sunk in the Battle of Guadalcanal.

Traer Salt and Pepper Shaker Gallery

You'll find one of the world's largest collections of salt and pepper shakers in Traer, south of Waterloo. You will see more than 16,000 pairs of shakers at the Traer Salt and Pepper Shaker Gallery.

The gallery features a collection that started in 1946 and has brought in many shakers from around the world. The shakers include modern and classic designs with some entertaining pairing arrangements. You will find animal-themed shakers, food-themed designs, and many rustic or rural-inspired models here.

Best Time to Visit:
The venue is open from April to November. You can visit outside that season, but you'll have to get an appointment.

Pass/Permit/Fees:
Admissions are $5 for adults and $1 for children.

Closest City or Town:
Waterloo

Physical Address:
411 2nd St, Traer, IA 50675

GPS Coordinates:
42.19393° N, 92.46897° W

Did You Know?
One of the sets you'll find here is the first one that the founder of the museum acquired in 1946 from the Brookfield Zoo in Chicago.

Briggs Woods Waterfall

Briggs Woods Waterfall is found in Briggs Woods Park outside of Webster City. It is an enjoyable area north of Des Moines that features multiple camping sites, an 18-hole golf course, and a few spaces for fishing. But the most popular part of the park is its waterfall. Briggs Woods Waterfall is around the northern end of the Briggs Woods Lake. The spillway is near the end of several trails. The waterfalls stretch out north and allow water to flow into the nearby Boone River. You can get great views of the waterfall from the Boone River Recreational Trail while you visit the area.

Best Time to Visit:
The spring season is a great time to visit since the trails won't be littered with as much debris from the nearby trees during that season.

Pass/Permit/Fees:
The park is open for free, but it costs extra to rent a campsite or play at the nearby golf course.

Closest City or Town:
Webster City

Physical Address:
2450-2498 Briggs Woods Rd, Webster City, IA 50595

GPS Coordinates:
42.43538° N, 93.79535° W

Did You Know?
The lake area offers spaces for fishing and swimming. These areas are separate from one another for safety.

Union Grove State Park

The Union Grove State Park in Gladbrook, Tama County, features more than 100 acres of land. It includes a waterfall, two boating ramps, and a swimming beach. You can also rent one of the campsites at the park if you wish. This park houses a few spots for fishing, particularly for angling.

The waterfalls at the park are noteworthy for featuring a straight-line design. The water flows evenly from the top and provides a smooth look throughout the entire area.

Best Time to Visit:
The park is open year-round, although the spring is the best and most temperate time to visit the park.

Pass/Permit/Fees:
The park is free to visit, but it costs extra to reserve a camping site here.

Closest City or Town:
Waterloo

Physical Address:
1215 220th St, Gladbrook, IA 50635

GPS Coordinates:
42.12501° N, 92.71847° W

Did You Know?
Some spots in the park include restored prairie surfaces. The prairie sites in the northeast corner of the park provide a peaceful space where you can see what the land looked like before settlement.

Grotto of the Redemption

The Shrine of the Grotto of the Redemption is one of the most unique buildings you will visit while in Iowa. This Roman Catholic shrine in the northwestern town of West Bend features nine grottos built with various minerals and petrified items. The fossils, shells, and other items were gathered and used in the construction of the grottos from 1912 to 1954.

The grottos feature depictions of various scenes in Jesus's life, among them the Stations of the Cross. Some ceramic statues also accentuate the mineral deposits throughout the area.

Best Time to Visit:
The grotto is open 24 hours a day. The local chapel at the grotto hosts masses on Sunday mornings.

Pass/Permit/Fees:
It is free to visit the grottos.

Closest City or Town:
West Bend

Physical Address:
208 1st Ave NW, West Bend, IA 50597

GPS Coordinates:
42.96402° N, 94.44573° W

Did You Know?
The grotto started after Father Paul Dobberstein became severely ill in 1897. He said he would build a shrine to the Virgin Mary if he survived.

Herbert Hoover National Historic Site

The Herbert Hoover National Historic Site in West Branch is a park built on the land where future President Herbert Hoover grew up from 1874 to 1885. The site features the cottage where he was born. There is also a blacksmith shop similar to the one his father owned, a small schoolhouse, and a Quaker meetinghouse where Hoover's family worshiped. The site is home to Hoover's final resting space. Hoover is buried next to his wife, First Lady Lou Henry Hoover. The Herbert Hoover Presidential Library and Museum is also near this historic site. The museum houses many exhibits about Hoover's presidency, including an exhibit dedicated to the Hoover Dam.

Best Time to Visit:
The site hosts special events around the anniversary of Hoover's birth on August 10.

Pass/Permit/Fees:
Admission is $10 for adults and $3 for children.

Closest City or Town:
West Branch

Physical Address:
110 Parkside Dr, West Branch, IA 52358

GPS Coordinates:
41.67242° N, 91.34589° W

Did You Know?
The area near Hoover's burial site features a tallgrass prairie similar to what people would have seen when settling in the area in the nineteenth century.

Bridges of Madison County

Only 6 of the 19 covered bridges of Madison County still exist. These bridges were prominently highlighted in the book *Bridges of Madison County* by Robert James Waller that was adapted into a film by Clint Eastwood. You can visit all six of these covered bridges while in Madison County. The Roseman Bridge near Winterset is the most prominent one, as it is believed to be haunted after a jail escapee in 1892 went through the bridge and was never found again. Other noteworthy bridges here include the Cedar, Cutler-Donahoe, and Hogback bridges. These are all near Winterset and feature distinct red wood bodies as they go over the Middle River. The bridges have become popular romantic getaway sites following the film's premiere in 1995.

Best Time to Visit:
The bridges are open to visit at any time.

Pass/Permit/Fees:
You can visit the bridges for free.

Closest City or Town:
Winterset

Physical Address:
2451 Elderberry Ave, Winterset, IA 50273

GPS Coordinates:
41.29340° N, 94.1459° W

Did You Know?
The oldest of these bridges is the Imes Bridge, which was built in 1870.

Clark Tower

You will find the Clark Tower in the southern part of Winterset in Winterset City Park. It is a castle-inspired limestone tower built in 1926. The tower is about 25 feet high and features a round staircase that goes outside to the top.

You can see much of the park area from the top of the Clark Tower. You'll find the Middle River to the south, while parts of Madison County Park appear to the west.

The tower's castle-like design features many small openings in the middle of its body, with a few points extending at the top.

Best Time to Visit:
You can visit the tower throughout the year.

Pass/Permit/Fees:
The tower is free to visit.

Closest City or Town:
Winterset

Physical Address:
2278 Clark Tower Rd, Winterset, IA 50273

GPS Coordinates:
41.32046° N, 94.00410° W

Did You Know?
The tower is named for Caleb and Ruth Clark, two of the first settlers of Madison County.

John Wayne Birthplace Museum

The town of Winterset is the birthplace of the iconic actor John Wayne. You can visit the John Wayne Birthplace Museum in the heart of the downtown area. The museum on John Wayne Drive is a block north of his original birthplace. The house and museum are open for tours throughout much of the year. You can see what life was like inside the Wayne household around the time of his birth in 1907. The museum features many artifacts highlighting Wayne's life and film career, including items used in some of Wayne's films, plus many outfits that he wore. You will also see items related to Wayne's family life and how he became a model of the American ideal.

Best Time to Visit:
The museum hosts a birthday celebration around May 26th of each year.

Pass/Permit/Fees:
Tickets are $15 for adults and $8 for children.

Closest City or Town:
Winterset

Physical Address:
205 S John Wayne Dr, Winterset, IA 50273

GPS Coordinates:
41.33309° N, 94.01297° W

Did You Know?
One of the highlights of the museum is an original painting of Wayne produced by Andy Warhol.

Proper Planning

With this guide, you are well on your way to properly planning a marvelous adventure. When you plan your travels, you should become familiar with the area, save any maps to your phone for access without internet, and bring plenty of water—especially during the summer months. Depending on the adventure you choose, you will also want to bring snacks and even a lunch. For younger children, you should do your research and find destinations that best suits your family's needs. Additionally, you should also plan when to get gas, local lodgings, and where to get food after you're finished. We've done our best to group these destinations based on nearby towns and cities to help make planning easier.

Dangerous Wildlife

There are several dangerous animals and insects you may encounter while hiking. With a good dose of caution and awareness, you can explore safely. Here is what you can do to keep yourself and your loved ones safe from dangerous flora and fauna while exploring:

- Keep to the established trails.
- Do not look under rocks, leaves, or sticks.
- Keep hands and feet out of small crawl spaces, bushes, covered areas, or crevices.
- Wear long sleeves and pants to keep arms and legs protected.
- Keep your distance should you encounter any dangerous wildlife or plants.

Limited Cell Service

Do not rely on cell service for navigation or emergencies. Always have a map with you and let someone know where you are and for how long you intend to be gone, just in case.

First Aid Information

Always travel with a first aid kit with you in case of emergencies.

Here are items to be certain to include in your primary first aid kit:

- Nitrile gloves
- Blister care products
- Band-aids - multiple sizes and waterproof type
- Ace wrap and athletic tape
- Alcohol wipes and antibiotic ointment
- Irrigation syringe
- Tweezers, nail clippers, trauma shears, safety pins
- Small Ziplock bags containing contaminated trash

It is recommended to also keep a secondary first aid kit, especially when hiking, for more serious injuries or medical emergencies. Items in this should include:

- Blood clotting sponges
- Sterile gauze pads
- Trauma pads
- Second-skin/burn treatment
- Triangular bandages/sling
- Butterfly strips
- Tincture of benzoin

- Medications (ibuprofen, acetaminophen, antihistamine, aspirin, etc.)
- Thermometer
- CPR mask
- Wilderness medicine handbook
- Antivenin

There is so much more to explore, but this is a great start.

For information on all national parks, visit: www.nps.gov.

This site will give you information on up-to-date entrance fees and how to purchase a park pass for unlimited access to national and state parks. This site will also introduce you to all of the trails of each park.

Always check before you travel to destinations to make sure there are no closures. Some hikes close when there is heavy rain or snow in the area, and other parks close parts of their land for the migration of wildlife. Attractions may change their hours or temporarily shut down for various reasons. Check the websites for the most up-to-date information.

Made in the USA
Las Vegas, NV
20 October 2024